Estate Planning
for Same-Sex Couples

JOAN M. BURDA

ABA General Practice, Solo & Small Firm Section

08 07 06 05 04   5 4 3 2 1

Burda, Joan M. 1952-
     Estate planning for same-sex couples / by Joan M. Burda
   Includes bibliographical references and index
   ISBN 1-59031-382-8
       1. Estate Planning 2.   Gay couples—Legal status, laws, etc.—United States   I.
             I. Title

   KF750. B87 2004
   346. 7305 ' 208664—dc22

                                                    2004015942

Discounts are available for books ordered in bulk. Special consideration is given to state bars, CLE programs, and other bar-related organizations. Inquire at Book Publishing, ABA Publishing, American Bar Association, 321 North Clark Street, Chicago, Illinois 60610.

www.ababooks.org

For Martha A. Webb, Ph.D.,
whose kindness and caring I can never repay.
Without you this book would not have been written.

Contents

About the Author ix

Acknowledgments xi

Introduction xiii

Chapter 1

Representing Lesbian and Gay Clients 1

An Underserved Population 1

Establishing a Niche Practice 2

Preliminary Considerations 3

Expanding a Practice to Include Lesbian and Gay Clients 4

Necessary Changes in Your Practice 4

Benefits of This Niche Practice 6

Chapter 2

**Understanding Legal Issues Affecting
Lesbian and Gay Clients** 7

General Issues 8

Same-Sex Couples Are Legal Strangers 9

Government Benefits Unavailable to Same-Sex Couples 11

Written Agreements between Same-Sex Couples 12

Children 13

Tax Considerations 13

Health Care Considerations 14

Elder Members of the Lesbian and Gay Community 17

Conclusion 18

Chapter 3

Agreements and Contracts 19

Domestic Partnership Agreements 21

Shared-Parenting Agreements 25

Chapter 4

Taxes and Trusts and Wills, Oh, My! 29

Wills 29
Prevalidating a Will 32
Designation of Heir Proceedings 32
Will Clauses to Include 33
Pets 34
Executor 34
Appointment of a Guardian 35
Trusts 36
Living Trusts 37
Testamentary Trusts 40
    Spendthrift Trusts 40
    Discretionary Trusts 41
    Pet Trusts 43
Charitable Remainder Trusts 45
Irrevocable Life Insurance Trusts 46
Taxes 47
    Gift Taxes 48
    Jointly Held Property 49
    IRAs 49
    State Death Taxes 49
Other Considerations 51
Conclusion 52

Chapter 5

Avoiding Probate 53

Standard Methods of Avoiding Probate 54
    Living Trusts 54
    Joint Tenancy 54
    Payable-on-Death Accounts 57
    Life Insurance 58
    Transfer-on-Death Vehicle Certificates 61
    Transfer-on-Death Deeds 61

Chapter 6

Children 63

Questions to Ask 65
Shared-Parenting Agreements 65
Second-Parent Adoption 66

Standby Guardian 68
Testamentary Provisions 68
Difficult Issues 69
"Psychological Parent" 70
Life-Planning Issues 71

Chapter 7
Essential Estate Planning Documents 73
Health Care Powers of Attorney and Living Wills 73
Designation of Agent 75
Funeral Arrangements 75
Guardian/Conservator Nomination 77
Durable Power of Attorney for Finances 77
Business Powers of Attorney 78
Government Accounts 79

Chapter 8
Lesbian and Gay Seniors 81
Older Americans Act 84
Nursing Home Care 85
Health Care Issues Affecting Lesbian and Gay Seniors 87
Social Security 88
Medicaid and Medicare 89
Insurance Concerns of Lesbian and Gay Seniors 92
Conclusion 93

Chapter 9
Other Issues and Considerations 95
Debts, Credit Reports, and Credit Cards 95
       Credit Reports 95
       Credit Accounts 97
Tax Returns 97
Social Security Benefits 98
Pension and Retirement Plans 98
Military Retired Pay 100
Nursing Homes, Retirement Communities, and Home Health Care .. 101
Foreign Same-Sex Marriages, Religious Same-Sex Marriages,
       and Civil Unions 102
Business Succession 104
Long-Term Care Insurance 104

Disability Insurance 105
Conclusion 105

Chapter 10
Finding and Marketing to the Gay Community 107
Have a Plan 108
Marketing to a Niche 109
Lesbian and Gay Legal Organizations 111
Educational Seminars 112
Write a Newsletter 113
Other Marketing Strategies 115
Teaching 116
Conclusion 116

Appendices
A: Estate Planning Forms 117
B: Resources 177

Index 191

About the Author

Joan M. Burda is a solo practioner in Lakewood, Ohio. In addition to her solo practice, Ms. Burda is the Program Director of the Cleveland Homeless Legal Assistance Program. This work involves developing programs to provide legal assistance to indigent persons. She is also an adjunct faculty member at Ursuline College in Ohio, where she teaches in the Legal Studies program.

Ms. Burda graduated from Bowling Green State University with a Bachelor of Liberal Studies degree. She received her J.D. from Pepperdine University School of Law. She was admitted to the Ohio Bar in May 1982.

Before attending law school, Ms. Burda spent three years on Capitol Hill in Washington, D.C. She was on the staff of Ohio Senator Robert Taft, Jr. and Indiana Congressman J. Edward Roush. She left Washington in 1976 to start law school in California.

This is Ms. Burda's second book for the General Practice, Solo and Small Firm Section. She published *An Overview of Federal Consumer Law* in 1998. A planned updating of that book is in process.

Ms. Burda is a member of the General Practice, Solo and Small Firm Section of the American Bar Association. She sits on that section's council. She is also a member of the editorial board of *GPSOLO*, the section's magazine. She has written for *GPSOLO* on issues involving child support, government benefit, and estate planning for non-traditional families.

Ms. Burda is a member of the Cleveland Bar Association, the Ohio State Bar Association, and the National Lesbian and Gay Law Association. She is a referral lawyer for the National Center for Lesbian Rights and the Lambda Legal Defense Fund.

She lives in Lakewood, Ohio with her partner of 14 years, Betsy Ashley, and their dog, Hershey.

Acknowledgments

Many people contributed to this book. At the risk of forgetting someone, I want to thank the following:

Jean Iverson, executive editor at the American Bar Association, has been an incredible resource from the ABA and the publishing point of view.

Jill Nuppenau developed the marketing campaign for the book. I learned a great deal from her about market expectations and how to meet them.

Elio F. Martinez, Jr., chair of the Publication Board for the General Practice, Solo and Small Firm Section, gave me much support and encouragement.

Corinne Cooper is my liaison with the ABA Publication Board. She helped arrange peer reviews of the manuscript. Her enthusiasm and interest in this project encouraged me during the writing process. Her suggestions and contributions allowed me to make the final product better.

Rick Paszkiet is my editor. My first meeting with him occurred at the 2004 Midyear Meeting. His suggestions, ideas, and recommendations are always on point. And, he read my first book . . . and liked it.

I am grateful to everyone on the General Practice, Solo and Small Firm Section's Publication Board for supporting this project. The issues covered in this book are on the cutting edge of the law. The board saw this as a developing issue and approved the book proposal. I hope the final product does not disappoint them.

The GPSSF staff at the American Bar Association is wonderful. Whenever I had a question someone always responded. No ABA member could get much done without this phenomenal group of people.

I also owe a debt of gratitude to my sister, Janet, for letting me use her computer to work on the book while I was on vacation in Colorado. Margaret Morgan, her program support assistant, helped me and I am grateful to her.

Several attorneys who practice in this area assisted me in developing the book's contents. They also generously provided forms they use in their practice. These are included in Appendix A. Susan Murray of Langrock, Sperry & Wool, LLP, of Middlebury, Vermont, explained the Vermont civil union law to me. She also gave me the name of the justice of the peace who officiated at my civil union ceremony.

Lisa Ayn Padilla, a partner in the law firm of Gibbons, Del Deo, Dolan, Griffinger & Vecchione in New York, provided information in several areas.

Matthew Dubois of Vogel & Dubois of Portland, Maine, discussed his practice and the concerns of his lesbian and gay senior clients. He is in the vanguard of attorneys addressing the needs of lesbian and gay elders.

Writing a book can be a tortuous endeavor. It challenges the strongest of relationships. I am fortunate to have a wonderful partner, Betsy Ashley. We celebrate fourteen years together in 2004. She supports and encourages me without reservations. No one could ask for more from a lifetime commitment together. On August 6, 2002, Betsy and I entered into a civil union in Middlebury, Vermont. I am grateful and humbled that she said "yes."

Finally, I want to thank Martha A. Webb. I am grateful for her support, her patience, and her confidence in my ability to get this done. And, as usual, she was right.

Introduction

Recently, the issues addressed in this book have taken a front seat in society. People have strong ideas and feelings about same-sex relationships. The idea for this book came to me several years before the current rage.

In August 2002, my partner, Betsy, and I entered into a civil union in Vermont. We knew our action would not be recognized outside of Vermont; however, it was important for us to publicly formalize our relationship. Many lesbian and gay couples face this decision. We do what we can to protect and formalize our relationships.

Lesbians and gay men pay taxes, buy homes, raise children, care for elderly parents, cut the grass, and walk the dog. Our lifestyle reflects that of our heterosexual neighbors. Our agenda is no different from anyone else's: life, liberty, and the pursuit of happiness.

This book is intended to provide estate-planning lawyers with an introduction to the issues faced by lesbian and gay clients. Many lawyers have lesbian and gay clients, but may not know it. In many cases, these clients are wary of revealing their sexual orientation to people with whom they have limited contact. That includes their lawyers. Yet, as attorneys, we need to know as much as possible in order to provide the services necessary to meet the client's needs.

The legal landscape concerning same-sex relationships is changing. On May 17, 2004, Massachusetts became the first state to grant same-sex couples the opportunity to enter into a legally sanctioned marriage under state law. On November 18, 2003, the Massachusetts Supreme Judicial Court ruled that banning same-sex marriage violates the Commonwealth's constitution.[1] The court gave the Massachusetts legislature 180 days to "take such action as it may deem appropriate."

That decision raised the issue of whether civil unions would be an acceptable alternative to marriage. The Massachusetts Senate submitted that question to the justices in order to clarify the matter. On February 3, 2004, the court issued its opinion. According to the majority of the justices, civil unions

---

1. Goodridge v. Dept. of Public Health, 440 Mass. 309, 798 N.E.2d 941, 2003 Mass. LEXIS 814 (2003).

are not synonymous with marriage. Civil unions would not be an acceptable alternative. The justices wrote, "The history of our nation has demonstrated that separate is seldom, if ever, equal."[2]

At this writing, the legislature is considering an amendment to the Massachusetts Constitution. The preliminary amendment will state that only a man and a woman can enter into "marriage." The amendment's proposed language will permit same-sex couples to enter into a civil union with most of the rights granted to married couples.

This is the first step in Massachusetts to amend the constitution. The process requires passage of the amendment by the legislature on two separate occasions before the measure is put to a public vote. That process will take at least two years. The court's decision took effect on May 17, 2004.

When same-sex marriage became a reality in Massachusetts on May 17, 2004, lesbian and gay couples in the Commonwealth were given the same inheritance rights as any other married couple. This change in Massachusetts law affects a plethora of legal rights, including family law and probate. The full extent of the effect will not be known for some time. Lawyers who represent lesbian and gay clients must, therefore, keep themselves apprised of these rapidly changing events.

Even if Massachusetts amends its constitution in 2006, the next issue involves the continued legal efficacy of the marriages people entered into under the court's decision. Can the state, after the fact, declare those marriages to be civil unions with reduced rights? A constitutional amendment in Massachusetts will create more legal uncertainty for those couples who marry over the next two years.

This decision permitting same-sex marriage means that lesbian and gay couples will be entitled to the protection of the same laws as heterosexual married couples. Another hurdle for couples marrying in Massachusetts will come when they leave the state and attempt to have their marriage recognized in other states. No one is sure if the U.S. Constitution's full faith and credit clause will apply.

Existing Massachusetts law does throw a monkey wrench into the plans of nonresident same-sex couples.[3] Current law states that a marriage license cannot be issued if the marriage will not be valid in the nonresidents' home state. This statute gives legal authority to Massachusetts authorities to refuse to issue a license to nonresident same-sex couples. There is no indication the

---

2. Opinions of the Justices to the Senate, 440 Mass. 1201, 802 N.E.2d 565, 2004 Mass. LEXIS 35 (Feb. 3, 2004), p. 9.
3. MASS. GEN. LAWS ch. 207, § 11 (1913).

law has been used before and there is no way to know if Massachusetts will invoke it in this situation.

The court's decision has prompted a backlash across the country that will continue for some time. Thirty-nine states have enacted legislation defining marriage as being between a man and a woman. These states claim their position is reflective of the strong public policy of the state. These states also believe such legislation preempts any argument under the full faith and credit clause. It remains to be seen if that argument will succeed. At least four states have amended their constitution to avoid a situation similar to Massachusetts's.

The objections to same-sex marriages are similar to the objections raised about abolishing slavery, giving women and African-Americans the right to vote, and repealing the miscegenation statutes that were common in many southern states well into the 1960s. Those laws were dismantled following the United States Supreme Court decision in *Loving v. Virginia*.[4]

The argument is being raised that marriage is a historical institution that must be protected. President George W. Bush supports a federal constitutional amendment that restricts marriage to a man and a woman. The proposed amendment also provides that no state constitution can be interpreted to hold otherwise.

This amendment will also prohibit any marital-like benefits from being granted to anyone else. The ramifications of this amendment are far-reaching and, as yet, unknown. The president's position is an example of the post-Massachusetts backlash. Many see the Massachusetts decision as a harbinger of more terrible things to come.

The Massachusetts decision makes the issues covered in this book all the more timely. Providing written protection to the relationships of lesbian and gay clients has never been more important. So far, no one is proposing to ban same-sex relationships or to deny lesbians and gay men the protection of all laws. Still, it is best to prepare for the worst and hope for better and more sane and rational times.

This book provides an overview of the issues and concerns facing lesbians and gay men. I hope attorneys and their clients find it helpful. The Appendices include forms and information that lesbian and gay clients and their attorneys can use to prepare a complete estate plan.

Married couples do not need all the documents discussed in this book. However, lesbians and gay men do need them because of the legal limbo in which they find themselves. In some cases, the documents lesbians and gay

---

4. 388 U.S. 1, 87 S.Ct. 1817. 18 L.Ed.2d 1010, 1967 U.S. LEXIS 1082 (1967).

men execute seek to memorialize the rights that heterosexual clients take for granted.

Attorneys who represent lesbian and gay clients must provide creative estate planning that protects both parties to the relationship, their children, and their future.

Elderly lesbian and gay clients present concerns that are even more serious. They are concerned about the care they will receive should they become incapacitated and are unable to remain in their homes. This is where a knowledgeable attorney becomes essential.

There is a significant lesbian and gay population in this country. The rules affecting lesbians and gay men are changing daily. We, as lawyers, must stay on top of those changes.

I hope this book provides a road map for attorneys to follow in advising their lesbian and gay clients.

Let me know what you think of the book. I'd like to know if it helps you and your clients.

Joan M. Burda
Lakewood, Ohio
jmburda@mac.com

Chapter 1

Representing Lesbian and Gay Clients

An Underserved Population

The Human Rights Campaign (HRC), a Washington, D.C.–based gay rights organization, estimates there are 3,136,921 same-sex households in the United States. This is based on a February 2001 Harris Interactive Poll showing that 30 percent of gays and lesbians live together in committed relationships. The HRC estimate differs significantly from the data released by the 2000 census. The 1990 Census offered the first opportunity for "unmarried couples" to be counted. The Census found that 145,130 same-sex couples lived in the United States. However, by all accounts, this data cannot be compared to the 2000 Census because of differences in collection and analysis.

The 2000 Census counted 601,209 same-sex couples living in the United States. HRC believes this is an undercount. One reason for that belief lies in the Census disregarding same-sex spouse responses. The 1996 Defense of Marriage Act (DOMA) requires that all federal agencies only recognize oppo-site sex marriages for purposes of any federal programs. Census data is used to determine allocation of federal resources. Therefore, the Census Bureau invalidated all same-sex spouse responses. The results are not comparable, however, because of the differences in collecting and processing the data in the 1990 and 2000 Census.

The 2000 census estimated the total U.S. population at 209,128,094. The HRC estimates the lesbian and gay population at 5 percent of that total.[1]

---

1. David M. Smith & Gary J. Gates, "Gay and Lesbian Families in the United States: Same-Sex Unmarried Partner Households: A Preliminary Analysis of 2000 United States Census Data" (Aug. 22, 2001), available at http://www.urban.org/UploadedPDF/1000491_gl_partner_households.pdf.

Some estimate that seven out of every ten lesbian and gay (LG) couples do not have the legal documents needed to memorialize their relationships and protect their assets. These numbers reflect the untapped client base available to attorneys interested in providing estate and life-planning services to LG couples.

Lesbians and gay men have special legal needs. All legal documents prepared for them are subject to court challenge. Legal documents valid in one state may be unenforceable in another state.

Establishing a Niche Practice

Individual lawyers, small firms, and some larger firms are beginning to see the value in marketing to gay men and lesbians.

The need for life and estate planning for LG clients is on the rise. This is a growing opportunity in estate planning if only because, like the rest of the population, LG baby boomers are getting older. In addition, there is the "gayby" boom: Lesbians and gay men are becoming parents in greater numbers. This creates additional opportunities in family law, including second-parent adoptions, foster care, artificial insemination, and surrogate parenthood.

Life planning for gay men and lesbians involves more than financial issues. Unlike heterosexual individuals or couples, LG couples need to document the very existence of their relationships. Nothing can be taken for granted. The current state of the law provides little protection for persons involved in nontraditional relationships.

Innovative lawyers can expand their practices by tapping into this client base. To establish a niche practice, the lawyer must determine not only the size of the competition but the size of the demand. There is a demand and opportunity for enterprising lawyers. Some lawyers see the benefits, personally and professionally, of concentrating their practice in certain areas. The gay community represents a source of clients to which an attorney can market legal services.

A niche practice also allows attorneys to get the highest value for their marketing budget. Limiting the scope of the marketing effort allows you to focus on the type of law practice you do best and in which you are most interested. Developing a reputation in a certain area, and advertising it, can result in referrals from other attorneys.

To date, major litigation involving gay men and lesbians has been handled by a variety of gay legal assistance groups such as the Lambda Legal Defense Fund and the National Center for Lesbian Rights. These organizations use their own legal staff and local counsel to bring cases. Local lawyers can benefit from the expertise and support of these organizations when representing gay and lesbian clients in ordinary matters.

Preliminary Considerations

Before deciding that this type of practice is for you, think about whom you will be representing. Before deciding to represent LG clients, you must first determine your own comfort level.

This is about more than tolerance; it is about acceptance. You will be using your skills and talents to represent clients many people find morally objectionable. Representing LG clients could have an adverse effect on your practice. This is a legitimate consideration.

Usually, the client is told to "go with your gut" when selecting an attorney. That is still true, but you must also decide whether you are comfortable dealing with LG clients. Be aware of your own feelings about gay men and lesbians. If the client senses hostility on your part, the client will be reluctant to be candid with you.

Many lesbians and gay men have experienced legal discrimination and societal ostracism. They may be reluctant to approach a professional and reveal their sexual orientation because they fear the consequences.

The hallmark of the attorney-client relationship is that it be open and honest. That is impossible if the attorney merely tolerates the person seated before her.

In an estate- and life-planning situation, clients deal with concerns, wishes, and desires closest to the heart. This is intensely personal and the client must feel safe with the attorney, safe enough to discuss the situation honestly and completely.

Clients may ask questions on the following issues:

1. Do you have experience dealing with sexual orientation or AIDS-related issues?
2. Have you represented other LG clients?
3. Do you have any personal doubts or issues about equal rights and treatment for LG clients with HIV or AIDS?
4. Are you familiar with legal arguments used against the interests of LG clients?
5. Are you comfortable seeking assistance from LG organizations?
6. Who will do most of the work?

Do not forget that getting into this niche will require you to change the way you look at your clients. While you will gain LG clients who are open about their relationships, you will also see clients who are not so open. You may find some married clients coming to you for a divorce, afraid to tell you that the reason for the break-up is their sexual orientation.

Expanding a Practice to Include Lesbian and Gay Clients

Gay and lesbian individuals and couples are looking for lawyers who understand their needs. Representing LG clients means dealing with unique legal issues.

On the surface, the issues appear to be similar to those faced by an unmarried heterosexual couple. The one major difference is this: With a couple of "I dos" and a signature on a piece of paper, that heterosexual couple automatically and immediately gains access to all the legal benefits and protections marriage has to offer. Gay men and lesbians do not have that option.

Although the legal landscape is changing, many states treat lesbians and gay men differently from heterosexuals under the law. This includes being excluded from intestate succession statutes and being denied the many protections of civil marriage contracts and family laws others take for granted. An example is Florida, which, though it does allow lesbians and gay men to be foster parents, explicitly prohibits them from adopting children.

The recent United States Supreme Court case *Lawrence v. Texas*[2] is significant because the Court, for the first time, legitimized the right to privacy in same-sex relationships. This decision may lay the foundation for sweeping legal change in the United States. The Court, in its decision, abolished criminal laws that singled out same-sex activities and restored the sanctity of a person's private life. This is an exciting time to be involved with these legal issues.

More recently, the Massachusetts Supreme Judicial Court ruled that the prohibition against same-sex civil marriage violates the Commonwealth's constitution and ordered the state to issue marriage licenses to same-sex couples beginning May 17, 2004.[3] This decision will make Massachusetts the first U.S. state to permit legally sanctioned civil marriages of same-sex couples.

Necessary Changes in Your Practice

The software on the market today dealing with estate planning does not address the unique issues presented by LG clients. For example, will-writing

---

2. 539 U.S. 558, 123 S.Ct. 2472, 156 L.Ed.2d 508, 2003 U.S. LEXIS 5013 (June 26, 2003).
3. Goodridge v. Dept. of Public Health, 440 Mass. 309, 798 N.E.2d 941, 2003 Mass. LEXIS 814 (2003).

software provides for married and unmarried persons, with and without children. LG couples in committed relationships are "unmarried persons" as defined by existing law. Although they lack a state-issued piece of paper, these couples are as married as anyone who stood before a judge or minister. Standard will-writing software requires that you cut and paste to make the language fit the situation faced by lesbian and gay clients.

You will need to customize the documents prepared for LG clients. There are no short cuts and there are few boilerplate clauses. This practice requires you to interact closely with your client and prepare documents that reflect the individual needs and wishes of the client. Appendix A contains many forms that you can use in your practice to meet your clients' needs.

Many of the estate documents used for LG clients overlap. The documents stand as a unified statement of the client's intent. Interconnecting the documents serves the client's desire to ensure the estate plan will be honored. It also discourages legal challenges to the plan's validity by unaccepting family members.

In order to raise the comfort level of prospective LG clients it is helpful to consider your office forms, staff attitude, décor, and even the publications in the waiting room. This is where a client's first impression is made. Such a review allows you to use your office environment as part of your marketing strategy.

Do not be surprised if a prospective client asks about your office employment policies, either directly or indirectly. Take the initiative and include "sexual orientation" in your firm's nondiscrimination policy. Post the policy in a conspicuous place. The same goes for providing health benefits for your employees' domestic partners. Most *Fortune* 500 companies are doing just that—because it makes good business sense. Implementing policies that reflect your belief in diversity and nondiscrimination will serve you well when marketing to the gay community.

You will find it helpful to review your form letters and standard mailings. Make your form letters (intake, retainer, client memoranda) gender neutral. This can be accomplished by inserting non-gender-specific words ("the client," "you," etc.). This may strike you as unduly politically correct, but it will serve to make all your clients more comfortable. It is also an inexpensive and subtle way to market your firm.

Local law schools may have an LG student association. This is an excellent source of ideas for making your office more diverse. It is also a way to publicize your firm to prospective associates and clients in a positive way.

The law office staff is an essential part of the practice. Anyone considering expanding a practice to include estate and life planning for LG clients must include the staff in that process. It is important to understand how your staff feels about marketing to the LG community. While each person on the staff is responsible for his or her attitude toward these clients, often negative perceptions are the result of ignorance rather than malice. These discussions will also allow you to determine which staff members will be assigned to work with LG clients.

Nothing can short-circuit an attorney-client relationship faster than an inhospitable staff encounter. If the staff is uncomfortable serving gay and lesbian clients, you will have difficulty attracting and retaining clients. In the alternative, a welcoming atmosphere can result in a long-term client relationship and word-of-mouth marketing that no amount of money can buy.

Benefits of This Niche Practice

It is easy to deal with clients who fit a specific pattern, who present a standard, cookie-cutter set of issues. With LG clients, you will be called upon to create legal documents that will not only benefit the client but can stand up to legal challenges. Protecting a client's assets and providing for estate and life planning needs can give you a renewed appreciation for the practice of law. Your skills and talents will be called into play and you will be rewarded with the knowledge that you did something positive.

Chapter 2

Understanding Legal Issues Affecting Lesbian and Gay Clients

Estate planning is of vital importance to lesbian and gay (LG) clients. These clients must be aware of the variances at play and address them accordingly.

The law makes no assumptions when addressing the legal needs of gay men and lesbians. In fact, there may be laws in your jurisdiction that expressly limit or restrict the rights of gay men and lesbians or that exclude them from legal protection.

In most states, same-sex couples have no automatic legal protection. Some states, including Vermont, Hawaii, and California, do provide legal protection. New Jersey recently joined this select group of states when its legislature approved, and the governor signed, a law providing financial benefits and legal rights to same-sex couples. The New Jersey legislation, like that in California, also includes unmarried heterosexual couples over the age of sixty-two in its provisions.

Massachusetts began issuing marriage licenses to same-sex couples on May 17, 2004. According to existing Massachusetts law, however, only Commonwealth residents are eligible to be married. Chapter 207, Section 11 of the General Laws of Massachusetts states:

No marriage shall be contracted in this commonwealth by a party residing and intending to continue to reside in another jurisdiction if such marriage would be void if contracted in such other jurisdiction, and every marriage contracted in this commonwealth in violation hereof shall be null and void.

There is no indication this statute has ever been invoked. However, it is on the books and any other state can use it as another reason to deny recognition of a marriage entered into in Massachusetts by a nonresident couple. Since no state in the Union recognizes same-sex marriages, any marriage entered into by a nonresident would be considered null and void.

All legal documents prepared by a same-sex couple are contestable in court. None of those documents contains the protection or benefits of a state-recognized and -sanctioned civil marriage. However, they can be supported on a contract theory, except, of course, those involving children.

Intestate succession laws, where the decedent's assets go to the heirs at law, are an example of exclusion. There are no provisions in these statutes for a decedent's same-sex partner. This is true without regard to the length of the couple's relationship or whether the decedent had any relationship with the heirs at law.

Courts in many states have ruled that the same-sex partner of the child's biological parent is not a stepparent. The result is that the same-sex partner is prevented from being legally recognized as a parent.

Vermont is the first state to provide equal rights for same-sex couples through civil unions. It is the one state that grants the same rights, responsibilities, and obligations to same-sex couples in a civil union as to heterosexual married couples. Children born to a same-sex couple who are joined in a civil union are recognized as the natural children of both parents.

Even though Vermont has taken steps to level the legal playing field, same-sex couples continue to face barriers when they leave that state's boundaries. For example, even though both partners may be considered under Vermont law to be a child's natural parents, there is no guarantee that another state will honor that recognition. Therefore, same-sex couples with children are encouraged to take advantage of Vermont's second-parent adoption statute. It is another piece of paper, but one that may alleviate problems throughout the country.

General Issues

Many LG clients will bring major concerns to the first planning appointment. They are concerned about who will receive their estate and how they can prevent family members from interfering with their partner's inheritance. In some cases, the clients may be estranged from their families. This must be discussed with the clients to ensure that it is considered when the documents are prepared.

Clients are also concerned about guaranteeing that their partner will make decisions for them if they become incompetent. They want to know the best way to provide for their partner, their children, and their extended family.

Individuals and couples will want to discuss their concerns about whom to trust and to whom they should leave their estate. For myriad reasons, LG clients—individuals and couples—must do more life and estate planning than heterosexual clients must do. Nothing in the law of most states protects the families that gay men and lesbians create. That is the attorney's task.

Many LG clients wait an inordinate amount of time before looking into estate and life planning. It is important to encourage the client to start the process well before retirement. It is estimated that only 5 percent of same-sex couples have wills, relationship agreements, or durable powers of attorney.

It is also important to determine if there are any health concerns. It is necessary to address these issues in documents prepared for the client. Lesbians and gay men are treated as individuals for Medicaid and Medicare purposes, even if they are in a long-term committed relationship. For that reason, long-term care insurance can provide a sense of security for LG individuals and couples.

Attorneys must also be aware of the open hostility faced by gay men and lesbians. By remaining mindful of the additional factors coming into play, an attorney can provide the best and most complete service to the client.

Same-Sex Couples Are Legal Strangers

Lesbian and gay clients want to protect their assets and their partners. They will also want to protect themselves and their partners from interference by other people, including family members. All of this must be kept in mind when discussing the client's plans.

Providing an estate plan for a gay man or a lesbian, either an individual or a couple, requires the attorney to remember what law does *not* apply. Here is a partial list of the areas in which same-sex couples are treated as legal strangers:

- Burial determination
- Claim to the body
- Medical decisions regarding treatment, placement, and providers

- Intrusive mental health decisions
- Organ donation
- Hospital, nursing home, and prison visitation
- Presumption of guardian or conservator
- Child custody, child support, and visitation
- Joint adoption or foster care
- Attorney-client privilege
- Wrongful death
- Separate maintenance or alimony
- Property division when relationship terminates
- Inheritance

Social Security benefits are *not* available to the client's surviving partner. Most private pension plans, and all government retirement plans, restrict survivor benefits to a "surviving spouse." The federal Defense of Marriage Act[1] provides that same-sex couples cannot receive any federal benefits.

Generally, state intestacy laws do not cover same-sex couples. Dying intestate usually results in the surviving partner being denied any right to inherit from the decedent's estate. The intestate decedent's heirs at law claim all assets in most states. For this reason it is essential that you be familiar with the probate code in your state.

The Supreme Court of Washington State held, in a unanimous 2001 decision, that an inequity results if the State's intestate succession statute is applied against same-sex couples.[2] The Court held "[e]quitable claims are not dependent on the 'legality' of the relationship between the parties, nor are they limited by the gender or the sexual orientation of the parties."

The case dealt with a same-sex couple involved in a committed relationship for twenty-seven years. Robert Schwerzler died intestate in 1995. He and Frank Vasquez shared a house, a business, and financial assets, but all assets were in Mr. Schwerzler's name alone.

Mr. Schwerzler's family challenged Mr. Vasquez's claim to any part of the estate. The decedent's siblings described Mr. Vasquez as a "housekeeper" and, therefore, not entitled to any part of the estate assets.

The Washington Supreme Court held that a "meretricious relationship" existed between the men, thereby entitling Mr. Vasquez to benefit from Washington's intestate succession statutes. The court noted that the term "meretricious relationship" is a term of art in Washington State. It is defined as "a

---

1. Pub. L. No. 104-199, 110 Stat. 2419 (Sept. 21, 1996).
2. Vasquez v. Hawthorne, 33 P.3d 735 (Wash. 2001).

stable, marital-like relationship where both parties cohabit with knowledge that a lawful marriage between them does not exist." Under this doctrine, unmarried heterosexual couples are given community property–like treatment when one partner dies. The court found that this doctrine applied to Mr. Vasquez and the decedent. The court remanded the case for an equitable distribution of the estate property.

The *Vasquez* case is one example of the lengths a surviving partner must go to when faced with an intestate situation and a challenge by the decedent's family. The courts seem willing to entertain creative resolutions to situations not envisioned by legislatures when they drafted intestate succession statutes.

Government Benefits Unavailable to Same-Sex Couples

In 1997 the General Accounting Office (GAO) prepared a report identifying federal laws that contain benefits, rights, and privileges contingent on marital status.[3] Congress requested the report in conjunction with the passage of the Defense of Marriage Act. The GAO identified marital status as a factor in 1,049 federal laws in the United States Code.

The GAO listed thirteen categories in which marital status affected rights, benefits, and privileges:

- Social Security and related programs, housing, food stamps
- Veterans' benefits
- Taxation
- Federal civilian and military service benefits
- Employment benefits and related laws
- Immigration, naturalization, and aliens
- Indians
- Trade, commerce, and intellectual property
- Crimes and family violence
- Financial disclosure and conflict of interest
- Loans, guarantees, and payments in agriculture
- Federal natural resources and related laws
- Miscellaneous laws

The GAO stated that its list is representative but not definitive.

---

3. GAO/OGC-97-16, Defense of Marriage Act, B-275860.

Given the extensive nature of these categories, attorneys must be able to create life and estate plans that bridge the deficiencies existent in the law. The GAO list addresses only federal laws—it does not address the problems inherent in state law.

State law issues include

- Inheritance
- Adoption
- Dissolution of the relationship
- Custody
- Support
- Visitation
- Hospital visitation
- Health care

Written Agreements between Same-Sex Couples

Attorneys representing LG clients must be ready to prepare a series of legal documents to provide as much protection as possible. Most of these documents are unnecessary for married heterosexual couples, but they are essential parts of a complete life and estate plan for LG clients.

This is not an exhaustive list, but it is a starting point. Each case is unique and must be handled according to the clients' needs, intent, and wishes.

- Domestic partnership agreement (living together arrangement)
- Health care power of attorney
- Living will
- Durable power of attorney for finances
- Co-parenting agreement
- Wills
- Trusts
- Nomination of guardian for an adult
- Nomination of guardian for a minor
- Hospital/nursing home/hospice/other health care facility visitation authorization
- Authorization for autopsy/disposition of remains/burial arrangements

These documents constitute the core of planning for LG clients. There are few standardized formats for these documents. Examples of these documents are included in Appendix A. Contract law, not family law, governs the interpretation of these documents.

A possible exception is a document that purports to establish parental rights because the child's best interests are a consideration. A family law court will determine issues of child support, custody, and parenting time.

Children

Children are, and will continue to be, an integral part of LG families. Most states have restrictions of some sort on adoptions, custody, and visitation that adversely affect same-sex parents.

Denying a child the benefits of two parents, even if both are of the same sex, runs counter to the professed intentions of protecting the child's best interests. Children who are denied the legal protection of both parents can then be denied financial support, inheritance rights, and Social Security benefits. These are considerations that need to be discussed when establishing a life and estate plan for same-sex parents.

Any estate documents that address the children's needs should include a discussion reflecting the parties' intent to protect the children's best interests. Since this is often a primary judicial consideration, such evidence can go far in protecting the parents' rights. It is important to include language that clearly establishes the partners' beliefs concerning the children.

However, when dealing with the biological child of one partner, it is advisable to have the other partner retain separate counsel to review the documents addressing parental rights. This will forestall a future challenge in which you find yourself in the middle. The states are divided on how they perceive and enforce these parenting agreements. Therefore, it is in the parties' best interests to bifurcate representation on this issue.

Tax Considerations

Attorneys must also be cognizant of the estate tax issues facing LG clients. These issues will be discussed in greater detail in Chapter 4 dealing with taxes. For now, consider that many LG clients commingle assets without considering the tax consequences. They have joint accounts, add names to real estate, and list each other as beneficiaries for 401(k) and pension accounts. Most never think about what the Internal Revenue Service will do.

For example, the IRS will consider jointly held property to be wholly in the decedent's estate unless the surviving partner can prove one-half ownership.

Married couples do not need to keep extensive records of their joint financial dealings. It is essential to impress upon your LG clients the need to keep definitive records for transactions consummated during the relationship.

Commingling funds may trigger gift and income taxes. The federal and state tax repercussions usually do not come into play until after death. For example, each person has a $1 million lifetime gift exemption. However, any gift that exceeds the established yearly amount (currently $11,000) must be reported on a federal gift tax return before April 15 of the following year. This gift is counted against the individual's $1 million lifetime gift cap.

As with most people, your LG clients may not be tax savvy and may, therefore, incur tax liability for what they think is an innocuous act. A primary example is when a couple decides to hold real estate jointly. When one partner places the other's name on the deed without proper consideration, a gift is made. That act triggers the gift tax issue most same-sex couples never think about.

Health Care Considerations

Many LG clients will want to discuss health matters. A growing number of private corporations offer domestic partner benefits to their employees. This includes health insurance.

However, the employee-partner is taxed on the health insurance benefits provided to her partner. The IRS considers the benefits to constitute income to the employee-partner. That does not happen to a married couple.

An increasing number of cities offer domestic partner benefits to their employees. These benefits are also considered income to the employee and will be taxed.

Clients, however, need to review existing domestic partnership benefits in light of state (and potentially federal) law that would restrict marriage-like benefits to heterosexual married couples. There is a chance that companies will be prohibited, by law, from offering benefits to their employees. This will depend on the state, or states, in which the company operates.

The estate and life plan needs to address health care concerns. This is particularly true if either partner has a life-threatening condition. In that situation, the estate plan may contain a special needs trust. These trusts are discussed in greater detail in Chapter 4.

In order to avoid conflict with the client's relatives, it is important for the parties to discuss, in advance, the decisions being made. Of course, this works only if the client is not estranged from his or her family. If estranged, the family may attempt to circumvent the health care documents being prepared. Estranged or not, the client should send notice, by certified mail, to the family advising them of the decision made. In this way the family is on notice that the documents exist, and the U.S. Postal Service receipt is proof of that notice.

It may be helpful to document the fact that the client has had no contact with the estranged family. Specify the amount of time that has passed. Include anecdotal information about any interaction between the client and the family. This may assist the client in arguing that the family has no right to make decisions. An argument can be made that estranged family members are not entitled to make any decisions that contradict those intentions expressed by the client in a signed document.

The attorney can arrange to videotape the client signing documents. Affidavits signed by individuals familiar with the client's intentions can also be helpful.

State law governs advance directives (living wills and health care powers of attorney). The instructions given by an individual, and reflected in a written document, can usually be challenged under strict conditions. These conditions are generally set forth in the state statute creating the advance directive protocol.

Generally, hospitals will honor the expressed, written instructions of an individual. However, that is not always true. For that reason, it is best to be as explicit as possible when drafting these documents.

Advance directives usually take the form of a living will and a health care power of attorney. Living wills permit individuals to express, in writing, their wishes concerning the type of medical care they want when they are no longer competent. This document establishes clearly and in writing what the person authorizes. It can include a do-not-resuscitate order and a limitation on the use of life-support systems. The more specific the person is concerning these wishes, the less there is left to chance. There is no argument that the patient did not express any preferences.

The health care power of attorney allows an individual to designate a person as the one responsible for making health care decisions when the grantor is no longer able to do so. The power of attorney becomes active when the grantor is in a permanently unconscious state or terminal condition from which there is no hope of recovery. The grantor's physician and another physician make this determination. Neither the living will nor the power of attorney is effective unless and until the grantor is no longer able to make his own health care decisions.

Many states have developed advance directive forms and they are convenient to use. However, this does not mean they can be treated in a cavalier fashion. The clients must be aware of the need for the documents and anticipate family challenges.

Clients may want to execute multiple copies of these documents, with an original signature on each document. Using blue ink to sign the documents prevents confusion between copies and originals. The client should provide a copy of the documents to her family doctor, the person named as the agent for health care decisions, and any hospital or health care facility upon admission.

Gay and lesbian clients will also have concerns about how they are treated by the health care profession. There are situations where a hospital or doctor refuses to accept, acknowledge, or honor a health care power of attorney or living will that names a same-sex partner as the decision maker. Hospitals are required to accept these documents but enforcement takes time, and in some cases time may be of the essence.

Many hospitals have policies that limit visitation to "immediate family only." Many do not include same-sex partners in that category. This is contrary to the national hospital accreditation standards published by the Joint Commission on Accreditation of Healthcare Organizations. JCAHO defines "family" as "The person(s) who plays a significant role in the individual's [patient's] life. This may include a person(s) not legally related to the individual."[4] You may want to provide a copy of these standards to your clients.

Lambda Legal Defense Fund initiated a lawsuit against the University of Maryland Medical System for preventing a patient's same-sex partner from seeing him. The plaintiff lost after a jury trial, because the jury could not find that he suffered any damages.[5]

In that case, Robert Daniel fell ill and was admitted to the hospital. Bill Flanigan, his partner, made hospital personnel aware that he was Mr. Daniel's agent for health care decisions. Mr. Daniel's medical records also contained this information. The hospital chose to ignore the designation and refused to permit Mr. Flanigan to be with Mr. Daniel. Mr. Flanigan was allowed in only after Mr. Daniel's mother and sister arrived. By that time, Mr. Daniel had slipped into a coma and subsequently died.

This is a situation where the couple did everything they could and it still was not enough. Remind your clients that there are no guarantees. Most gay

---

4. JOINT COMMISSION RESOURCES, 2001 HOSPITAL ACCREDITATION STANDARDS, p. 322.
5. Flanigan v. University of Maryland Medical System, (Md. Cir. Ct., Baltimore City.) available at http://www.lambdalegal.org.

men and lesbians are well aware of that fact, but it is the attorney's job to remind them of the differences between legal rights and actual practices.

The United States Supreme Court ruled in *Cruzan v. Director, Missouri Dept. of Health*[6] that every individual has a constitutional right to direct his or her own medical care. To that end, it is imperative that the directions be clear, in writing and provided to the doctor and other medical personnel. It is useful to include specific instructions in the health care power of attorney and living will concerning the type of care desired, the type of care that is not to be provided, and other instructions that will set forth the individual's state of mind. Clients may also want to include a request that the grantor's wishes be respected and followed. The client may also want to designate the partner as the patient's agent for hospital visitation, receipt of personal property, and disposition of remains. Appendix A includes a "Designation of Agent" form that can be adapted for this purpose. The document should also include explicit language about releasing medical records that complies with the requirements of the Health Insurance Portability and Accountability Act (HIPAA). A sample form for the release of medical information is included in Appendix A.

Medical expenses can create financial stress for some clients. These clients may need to learn about financial alternatives available to them. Some clients may want to discuss viatication as part of their estate plan. This involves the sale of the client's life insurance policy to a company that pays the client a lump sum; the viatical company then assumes ownership of the policy.

Other alternatives include receiving financial support from family members, "living benefits," or "accelerated benefits." Reverse mortgages may also be an option for clients facing financial difficulties.

Elder Members of the Lesbian and Gay Community

Sexual orientation is not an issue that has come up to any degree in elder care. It is only a matter of time before it does. Aging gay boomer couples will want to stay together. The question is whether the care facility will recognize their right to do so. Neither state nor federal law addresses this issue. Litigation involving nursing homes and other health care providers who deny joint living arrangements will be filed in the not-too-distant future under fair housing or equal protection theories.

---

6. 497 U.S. 261 (1990).

Attorneys representing LG clients need to be aware of these options. Prepare for long-term care when discussing estate and life planning issues with clients. Some financial planners, such as American Express Financial, offer long-term insurance plans that do not discriminate against same-sex couples.

Conclusion

This chapter gives a summary overview of the types of legal issues faced by LG clients. It by no means exhausts the possibilities. When representing LG clients, attorneys must keep in mind the role society plays in relationships. Estate and life planning for LG clients requires creativity and innovation. Attorneys must strive to draft the most inclusive and protective documents possible. It is an opportunity to use the law for the benefit of the client when the law itself provides no specific protection.

Chapter 3

Agreements and Contracts

The face of the American family is changing in dramatic fashion. In time state legislatures will need to make the necessary changes in state law to protect all families, not just those that meet a traditional definition.

The agreements discussed in this chapter provide the means to create a complete life-planning package for your clients. Most lesbian and gay (LG) couples do not have formal agreements concerning their relationship. This often results in problems when the relationship ends either by death or separation. Using the documents referenced in this chapter will allow you to assist your clients in creating binding contracts that reflect their intentions concerning their relationship.

This is particularly helpful in the event that estranged family members challenge a surviving partner's rights to the decedent's estate. LG clients can use a variety of agreements to protect their relationship and their assets.

A formal, written agreement can provide LG couples with some measure of legal protection and recognition of their relationship. These documents give the couple the opportunity to manage their assets and plan for death and disability.

The legal system provides no protection if the partners fail to make their choices and intentions known. State laws are based on a traditional family structure in which members are related by blood or marriage. As a result, lesbian and gay relationships are excluded from the start.

Some states have enacted civil rights laws that include LG persons. They include California, Connecticut, Minnesota, and Wisconsin. These states have enacted laws that extend to lesbian and gay persons legal protection in the areas of employment, housing, credit, and public accommodations. In 2000, Vermont became the first state to codify civil unions.

In January 2004, the New Jersey legislature approved a bill granting gay couples many of the rights enjoyed by heterosexual married couples. This makes New Jersey the fifth state to recognize domestic partners. The New Jersey law provides that domestic partners shall have access to medical benefits and insurance and other legal rights. The state also recognizes partnerships granted in other states. Businesses will not be required to provide health coverage to same-sex partners of their employees. Insurance companies, however, will be required to make the coverage available. The law also allows surviving partners property rights and other survivor benefits.

In Vermont, couples who are joined in civil union benefit from most of the rights granted by the state to married couples. This includes the right to intestate succession, preference in naming a legal guardian, hospital visitation rights, transfer of property between partners without paying a transfer tax, and standing to sue for wrongful death and other types of injury cases if the partner is injured or killed.

While a couple need not be Vermont residents to be joined in civil union, no other state recognizes the union. As a result, the dissolution of a civil union outside of Vermont can be problematic.

The recent United States Supreme Court decision in *Lawrence v. Texas*, discussed in Chapter 1, is viewed by many as the vehicle through which same-sex relationships can receive greater access to civil benefits that are currently limited to heterosexual marriages.

In 2002, registered domestic partners in California began to enjoy expanded legal rights and protections as a result of Assembly Bill 25. The law makes registered domestic partners (same-sex and opposite sex) eligible for a plethora of legal protections. A partial list of those rights follows:

- The right to sue for the wrongful death of a partner
- Adoptions under the state's stepparent adoption procedures
- The right to make health care decisions for an incapacitated partner
- The right to claim state income tax deductions
- The right to claim an exclusion for a partner's medical care and benefits
- The right to be appointed administrator of the deceased partner's estate

The Massachusetts Supreme Judicial Court's decision in *Goodridge* held that prohibiting same-sex couples from civil marriage violates the Commonwealth's constitution.[1] The court ordered the state to issue marriage licenses to same-sex couples beginning May 17, 2004.

Those who believe their rights are being adversely affected sometimes attack the legal documents described in this chapter and throughout the book. Challenges are also mounted by estranged family members who disapprove of, or refuse to accept, the decedent's sexual orientation and his or her relationship. Estranged family members often rise up like a tsunami wave to claim their "right" to the property of their lesbian or gay relative.

The primary means used by disgruntled family members in challenging any document is to deny that the decedent was gay and to deny that there was an intimate relationship between the decedent and the surviving partner. These arguments can find a sympathetic ear from a judge who shares the family's distaste for same-sex relationships.

Written documents can alleviate this problem by creating a paper trail showing a long-standing desire by the parties to be considered a couple. It is also difficult to challenge a will when there is no evidence of mental incompetency, duress, undue influence, or fraud.

Because of the potential for challenges, gay and lesbian couples have a strong incentive to consult an attorney. They are looking for an attorney who is knowledgeable, comfortable about gay and lesbian issues including those involving HIV and AIDS, and eager to help them find creative solutions to their legal problems.

Samples of the agreements described in this chapter are included in Appendix A and on the accompanying CD-ROM.

Domestic Partnership Agreements

Lesbian and gay couples often use domestic partnership or "living together" agreements to describe the parameters of the relationship. These are similar to prenuptial agreements. They are rarely executed prior to the beginning of a relationship. In this respect lesbian and gay couples are not unlike their married counterparts.

When one partner supports the other or if there is a significant commingling of financial assets, a domestic partnership agreement is recommended. This agreement includes a disclosure of assets, provisions concerning the allocation of future property acquisitions, and provisions for current and future

---

1. Goodridge v. Dept. of Public Health, 440 Mass. 309, 798 N.E.2d 941 (2003).

support. The agreement should also contain a protocol for resolving disputes, including the dissolution of the relationship and the division of assets. This can include mediation, arbitration, or litigation. An agreement on costs and attorney fees is also advisable.

A domestic partnership agreement is the closest a same-sex couple can come to providing for their property interests. Contract, not family, law governs same-sex relationships.

Vermont, by virtue of its civil union law, legally recognizes same-sex couples. California's new domestic partner law also recognizes couples that register. Unlike Vermont, California's law also permits unmarried heterosexual couples to register if one of the partners is sixty-two or older. This recognizes the fact that seniors can lose pension and other benefits if they enter into a second marriage.

A same-sex couple can use these contracts to define their relationship. The parties can use the agreement to identify their finances and assets and specify how matters will be managed and by whom. The agreement also recites the parties' responsibilities and obligations in the relationship. This could include any specific duties assumed by either partner.

Further, the domestic partnership agreement includes an agreed-upon procedure for dissolving the relationship and providing for the division of the assets. Since this is a contract, it is important to discuss the consideration required to establish a binding contract between the parties.

Because these agreements are governed in contract law, the courts, not the legislature, govern their enforcement. It is unlikely any state legislature will attempt to restrict an individual's ability to enter a contract merely because of the sexual orientation of the parties.

These agreements are useful in describing the ownership status of the property brought into the relationship as well as property accumulated during the union. This can be particularly important if there is a significant difference in the financial status of the partners.

For example, one partner may be in school while the other is well established in a career. Or, one partner may own a house when the parties meet, and they elect to live in that house. A domestic partnership agreement gives the parties a vehicle through which they can address these issues.

Agreements that specify a sexual relationship as the sole consideration for the agreement can result in a court declaring the agreement unenforceable as against public policy. A sexual relationship in and of itself may not invalidate the entire contract. It is, however, important to include other considerations in the contract.

In 1981, a California appellate court refused to enforce a written agreement because it explicitly referred to sex in exchange for assets. The court construed the agreement to be one of prostitution.[2] The leading case in this area continues to be *Marvin v. Marvin*.[3] In that case, the California Supreme Court held that an agreement could not be based on "meretricious sexual services." But it is important to note that the court enforced the contract based on other considerations.

Some courts refuse to enforce domestic partnership agreements because the judge decides the parties' relationship is immoral. A Georgia trial court refused to enforce a domestic partnership agreement because of the parties' "illegal and immoral"[4] relationship. The Georgia Supreme Court reversed because the agreement did not require sexual activity.

In another California case, the court struck the reference to sex and enforced the contract.[5] That court saw the reference as a severable clause. Including a clause that the entire agreement does not fail if a court determines one or more paragraphs to be in violation of the law is a legitimate way to handle potential challenges. Clearly, reciting other considerations is key.

The *Lawrence* decision will also have an impact on these agreements. Specifically, the Georgia decision would not stand because the parties' relationship would be deemed irrelevant and immaterial to the enforceability of the contract.

It is advisable to identify the parties as "partners" or "domestic partners" and not "lovers." There is no standard lexicon for how LG couples describe each other. However, using the word "lovers" focuses attention on just one aspect of any intimate relationship.

The best agreement is one that clearly reflects the parties' intent and is written in plain, functional, and comprehensive English. The agreement should

- Identify the parties
- State the consideration for the contract
- Describe jointly held property, if any
- Include a provision for gifts between the parties
- Describe the parties' current residence (may duplicate description of jointly held property)

---

2. Jones v. Estate of Daly, 122 Cal. App. 3d 500 (1981).
3. 18 Cal. 3d 660 (1976).
4. Crooke v. Gilden, 414 S.E.2d 645 (Georgia, 1992).
5. Whorton v. Dillingham, 202 Cal. App. 3d 447 (1988).

- Describe any other real property owned, separately or jointly, at the start of the relationship
- Provide for the dissolution or termination of the relationship through appraisals, refinancing, and procedures to establish current fair market value of property
- Include a separate property schedule for each party
- Provide for the death of either party during the relationship or during the process of dissolving the relationship
- Include a full disclosure provision
- Include confidentiality and privacy provisions
- Provide for changed financial circumstances and how they affect the financial agreement of the parties
- Provide for mediation and/or nonbinding or binding arbitration
- Describe personal property brought to the relationship
- Describe inherited or gifted property received during the relationship
- State the allocation of individual and household expenses
- Include a clause requiring counseling before terminating the relationship
- Provide for custody, visitation, and support for any pets

Appendix A contains examples of domestic partner agreements that incorporate these different issues.

Specifying the process for dissolving the relationship through mediation or arbitration is important. Litigation is expensive. As the attorney, you are in a good position to explain the advantages of mediation and arbitration over litigation. Specifying the procedure, and the entity to be used, can save time and aggravation. The American Arbitration Association, for example, will not conduct an arbitration unless the agreement has an arbitration clause.

The agreement can provide for litigation, but you may want to include a provision that mediation or arbitration be attempted first. The parties can also agree to binding arbitration or, at least, mandatory nonbinding arbitration before entering the litigation nightmare.

Collaborative law is another vehicle available to the parties. This concept stipulates that the attorneys representing the individual parties agree to work on resolving the situation outside of court. The parties agree to not file legal action against each other. If an agreement is not possible the attorneys withdraw and the parties must retain new counsel and start from scratch. Collaborative law is not a widely used method of resolution, but it is a growing area of practice in family law.[6]

Often when a couple gets together one of them owns a house. It is not unusual for the other partner's name to be added to the mortgage and deed at some point. The agreement should contain a provision on how that is to be accomplished. The couple will need to understand the ramifications of adding a name to real estate and whether the goal can be accomplished with other means, such as a transfer on death deed, testamentary disposition, or a living trust. It is also important to address the possible gift tax consequences that arise in these situations.

Domestic partnership agreements are also helpful when real property is involved. Without an agreement the only way to remove someone's name from the deed is through a voluntary sale or a forced partition action. Either way the costs involved will exceed those charged for an agreement.

Shared-Parenting Agreements

The LG community experienced a "gayby" boom in the 1990s, when the number of LG parents increased dramatically. Unfortunately, there was also a similar rise in the number of contested custody, visitation, and support cases involving the children of those relationships. Some states permit "second parent" adoptions, while in others individual judges are known for granting them, even when there is no explicit law, since there is no one to object.

It is important to note that even when a second-parent adoption is granted by one state, a different state may refuse to recognize the order. Obviously, the full faith and credit clause of the U.S. Constitution comes into play, but it can be ignored under an argument of "state's rights" if a state has proclaimed a public policy against recognition of such actions. Clients must be made aware of all these possibilities and given an opportunity to plan for them.

Shared-parenting agreements can serve the purpose of providing the nonbiological parent with specific rights and responsibilities toward a child. These rights may not be provided for in state law and there is no guarantee that a court will uphold the agreement. This is true even if the child's best interests would be served by enforcing the agreement. Specifying rights does provide support for the nonbiological parent in the event the parties break up

---

6. See Pauline Tesler, Collaborative Law: Achieving Effective Resolution in Divorce without Litigation (ABA, 2001) for an explanation of the benefits of collaborative law and how it can benefit attorneys and their clients.

and an attempt is made to prevent the child from continuing a relationship with that person. The biological mother can use the standard family laws to prevent her former partner from having any relationship with the child. As you can imagine, this can be a sticky situation.

While a shared-parenting agreement cannot prevent an acrimonious split, it will make the parties think about the children's best interests during a time when the relationship is going well.

A shared-parenting agreement should include the following:

- Appointment of the biological parent's partner as the child's guardian. This is especially important since most courts will adhere to the mother's wishes.
- A clause granting power to the nonbiological parent to approve medical treatment for the child. This avoids delays in an emergency when the child requires care and medical personnel balk because "you're not the mother." This clause serves the child's health and welfare.
- Co-parenting clauses that provide for the care of the child.
- A provision that reflects the parties' decision concerning custody, visitation, and support.

In some cases, the identity of the other biological parent is known and that person intends to be involved in the child's life. It is important to discuss this scenario with your clients. Include the provisions for such involvement in a written document that will be signed by all affected parties.

For example, gay male couples that want children will sometimes use a surrogate. This allows one to fertilize the egg and become the child's biological parent. There are times when the surrogate mother, in agreement with the biological father, intends to be involved with the child. This situation requires specific contractual language that reflects the parties' intent and the accompanying rights and responsibilities.

A surrogate is the child's biological mother. Therefore, that person, unless she relinquishes all parental rights, can seek full custody from a court. The usual argument is the "best interest of the child." That may mean that a court awards custody to a surrogate over the father because of the father's sexual orientation or his relationship.

Some lesbian couples look to a friend or family member as the sperm donor. There should be a written agreement between the donor and the mother specifying each party's rights, responsibilities, and obligations. The donor can agree to relinquish all parental rights to the child in exchange for which the birth mother agrees that the donor is not responsible for paying child support.

It is important that an attorney draft this type of agreement and that all parties be represented by counsel. The potential for challenges in the future is all too real and can be harmful to the child.

The enforcement of such an agreement is not assured. Many jurisdictions will not allow a custodial parent to waive future child support. Also, the donor may return, at a later date, to demand parenting time with the child. This is all the more reason to ensure that counsel represents all parties.

As with the earlier example, the couple needs to discuss how parental rights, custody, support, and visitation will be handled. Too many LG couples rely on verbal agreements to control these situations. Inevitably, those unwritten promises result in controversy. A written agreement will reflect the parties' mutual understanding.

Some state courts allow visitation by the nonbiological parent, particularly when there is a close relationship with the child. Some courts have ordered the nonbiological parent to pay support. The legal landscape in this area is changing. For this reason alone, lawyers must be able to draft a comprehensive and clearly stated parenting agreement. Even though the law is in a state of flux now, there is no question that the courts are considering these relationships, and the children in them, with greater frequency.

In states that permit second-parent adoptions, like New York and Vermont, shared-parenting agreements are losing favor. Where second-parent adoptions are possible, the parties receive greater legal protection for the family they are creating. They should be encouraged to take advantage of the opportunity.

Shared-parenting agreements can be executed prior to or after the conception or birth of a child. The agreement can contain provisions concerning insemination and adoption costs and maternity costs as well as the daily financial issues. Child care must also be explored. Some agreements include an arbitration or mediation clause. Since the general rule is "best interests of the child," the clients must understand that such a clause may not be enforceable.

The agreement must also address tax issues including who claims the child as a dependent. In some cases, this includes the designation of "head of household." The child's health insurance will usually be the responsibility of the biological parent. This can change if a company that grants domestic partner benefits employs the nonbiological parent. However, there may be additional tax consequences to the nonbiological parent since the health benefits may be taxed as income.

The more specific the agreement, the better the chance that the parties have discussed the issues in detail. Sometimes writing things down brings matters into the light and allows the parties to review their thoughts and feelings.

Chapter 4

Taxes and Trusts and Wills, Oh, My!

Wills

Wills are the linchpin of every estate plan. Wills enable people to express their wishes concerning the disposition of their estate after death. Through a will one can provide for family and nonfamily members. It is a powerful document that allows a decedent to speak from the grave.

Without a will, the client's estate passes through intestate succession. A lesbian or gay couple cannot automatically inherit from each other. Intestate succession statutes are designed to provide for the distribution of estate assets to immediate and, down the line, not so immediate relatives. This makes the need for a will of incredible importance.

Vermont's civil union law created a vehicle through which same-sex couples can enter a legally recognized relationship. Vermont couples joined in a civil union are entitled to the protection of virtually all laws that have traditionally benefited married couples. This includes being covered by the Vermont intestate succession statute.

As of July 1, 2003, California permits registered domestic partners to be included in its intestate succession statute. This entitles the surviving partner to be treated in the same way as a surviving spouse. To enjoy this benefit couples must register with the California Secretary of State.

The Massachusetts Supreme Judicial Court's decision in *Goodridge*[1] determined that the Commonwealth's constitution gives same-sex couples the right

---

1. Goodridge v. Dept. of Public Health, 440 Mass. 309, 798 N.E.2d 941 (2003).

to enter into a civil marriage. The legal landscape is changing, although how much is still in question.

Because lesbian and gay (LG) couples are not recognized in the majority of states, it is necessary for them to create legal documents detailing their relationship. Preparing these written documents concerning the shared relationship can be complex and overwhelming for the client. It is the attorney's job to explain the benefits and advantages of drafting a complete estate plan.

The legal documents you prepare for your clients help control the disposition of their assets. It also gives them the opportunity to spell out for everyone who and what is important to them.

Many LG couples are already in some form of a contractual relationship. Preparing the legal documents does not negate the emotional feelings they share. Rather, the process allows them to formalize, in their own minds, just what they want done.

In many cases, assets can be held jointly thus precluding the need to provide for those assets in a will. However, there are other assets that cannot be jointly titled and must be provided for in a written, legally recognized document. Without a will, the individual's family will inherit and the surviving partner will be left out in the cold.

It is not unusual for a lesbian or gay couple to hold all or most of their property separately. In many cases, the house is held in the name of one party through a warranty deed. This means the house must pass through probate and a will is needed if the property owner wants his or her partner to inherit the house. Without that will, the house will be part of the intestate estate and pass to the decedent's surviving relatives.

A Florida example is pertinent. A gay couple enjoyed a committed relationship for years; however, the house, property, bank accounts, and other assets were in the name of only one partner. That man became ill and died, without a will.

Following the funeral, the decedent's family encouraged the surviving partner to take a walk on the beach. While he was gone the family changed the locks, emptied the contents of the house, and took the couple's dog to an animal shelter in another county. When the surviving partner returned he was told the house was not his, he could no longer live there, and everything in it belonged to the decedent's family—including his own clothing. The family also refused to tell him where they had taken his dog. The entire scenario could have been avoided had the parties executed wills or other documents providing for the disposition of the estate. Horror story? Yes, and one that is not unique.

Most people do not like thinking about wills. Many people believe they will die if they execute a will. Irrational? Perhaps, but such thoughts are undeniably part of the process. Further, you will hear excuses such as, "I'm too young," "I don't need a will because I don't have a lot of money or property," and "I cannot afford a lawyer."

Standard will language, required by your jurisdiction, is the start of preparing adequate estate documents for your clients. There are also a number of other considerations that you must address. Many LG clients are estranged from all or part of their families. They are concerned that family members will show up and contest the will. Many people believe that wills are easily contested. They may need to be told that will contests can be based on fraud, duress, incompetence, or undue influence, but the burden of proving any of these factors rests with the contesting party. If that burden cannot be sustained, the contest fails.

When clients intend to leave biological family members out of their wills they should include written statements about their intentions. This can be included as a clause in the will or as a separate statement attached to the will. Including a specific clause can remove evidentiary problems should the will be contested. Setting forth the testator's reasons for her actions in the will may alleviate a potential contest.

Another reason for including an express provision involves the possibility of a future action against the testator's attorney. Case law in some states permits unhappy heirs to sue the testator's attorney. This possibility can be preempted by including specific language identifying the heirs, or class of heirs, who are not provided for in the will. With the exception of spouses and children, no one is entitled to share in anyone's estate. Still, providing specific language will benefit the testator, the named beneficiary, and the drafting attorney from a frivolous lawsuit.

Some LG couples want to execute mirror wills—both wills, except for the names, are identical. It is important that the alternate residue clauses in both wills are identical. There may be no children and the parties may be unknown to each other's biological family.

When a same-sex couple has children and the nonbiological parent has not adopted the children, it is important to define the relationship the nonbiological parent has with the partner's biological children. Such a definition clause is also important in adoption situations when second-parent adoptions are not possible. If one party is pregnant when the wills are drafted, use a clause that includes the partner's children and their descendants. It is also possible to define "children" to include those who are being adopted, even if the proceedings are not completed before the testator's death. In essence, you are trying to cover all the bases to preempt a dispute over what the testator meant and whom she intended to include.

Lawyers should keep detailed notes in the file about client statements, office discussions, and attorney observations concerning any decision to leave out biological family members.

Prevalidating a Will

There are some steps an attorney can take to avoid potential will challenges. For example, Ohio state law provides for a hearing to prevalidate a will. This proceeding allows testators, during their lifetime, to ask the court to determine whether their will is valid. All parties entitled to notice under the Ohio Descent and Distribution statute are notified of the hearing and permitted an opportunity to appear and contest the will. A finding by the court that the will is valid precludes any will contest when the testator dies. After the hearing the will is filed with the probate court. Should the testator change the will, the procedure must be repeated.

This process permits the testator to give notice to the family of his intentions. The family is given the opportunity to contest the will on the basis of fraud, duress, incompetence, or undue influence. Failure to meet that burden results in the finding of the will to be valid. If the court finds that there is evidence of duress, fraud, incompetence, or undue influence, the will presented for validation is declared invalid. The testator can then take the necessary steps to draft a new will that will survive a contest. At that time the testator can return to court to seek validation of the new will.

Challenging a will under these circumstances would be difficult. The fact that the testator is seeking prevalidation would in itself preclude a finding of fraud, duress, incompetence, or undue influence.

It may be possible to seek prevalidation even if your state does not have a specific statute. A petition to prevalidate a will is a preemptive move on the part of the testator. Will contests take place after death, and prevalidation is a request to move up the contest to a time when the testator can provide evidence of his state of mind.

Designation of Heir Proceedings

Some states also allow a person to file a petition with the probate court to have a certain person designated as an heir. When this is accomplished, the designated person becomes an heir entitled to inherit under the laws of intestate succession.

As with the prevalidation of a will, this proceeding allows a testator to give notice to all other prospective heirs of his intentions concerning the disposition of his estate. The heirs are given an opportunity to appear and contest the designation.

Will Clauses to Include

Clients may be reluctant to go to the expense and trouble of designating an heir or prevalidating the will. Others may believe that the chance of a will contest is slim. In those cases, clients can be offered the opportunity to include a clause that sets forth why they are taking the action they are.

For example, an *in terrorem* clause may be included to provide that anyone contesting the will is to receive nothing from the estate. This is best accomplished by leaving a bequest of such significance that the potential contestant thinks twice before initiating any action. Further, the clause can include a provision that authorizes the executor to pursue attorney fees and costs in any will contest. The clause can also provide that any expense incurred in defense of a will contest is to be deducted from the contestant's testamentary share of the estate.

A will can also include a clause that sets forth the testator's reasons for disposing of her estate in the way she did. This clause can include language such as

> Debra Smith is my life partner. We have been together since October 1, 1982, in a committed and loving relationship. In 2002, we entered into a civil union in Middlebury, Vermont. We would have married in a civil ceremony had the law allowed.
>
> I leave my estate to Debra, my life partner of more than twenty years. I do not do this out of any disrespect or lack of love or affection for my family. Rather I do so because she is the person I love and with whom I have spent my life. We shared our lives together. I expressly intend to benefit her. She has been a source of great love, comfort, and companionship to me. I believe my family is adequately cared for and does not need any support from me. I ask my family to recognize the commitment that Debra and I share and to accept my wishes expressed in this will.

Such a clause serves as evidence of the testator's intent. This can be an invaluable tool should a family member contest the will. Too often, families come into the picture after death and argue that the couple was not getting along, that the decedent was not gay, or that they were "just roommates." Written documentation attesting to the relationship and its length can refute these allegations.

Another clause can exclude anyone from receiving a part of the estate who has had no contact with the testator for a specified period. The clause can designate a period of time immediately preceding the testator's death. There are many cases where decedents were estranged from their families, yet upon their death the families showed up to collect their due.

There is no guarantee that a court will enforce these clauses, and the clients must be made aware of that possibility. However, these clauses do provide written documentation that the testator considered the issue when drafting the will. This is another reason why the boilerplate language does not work for LG clients.

Pets

Clauses affecting the disposition of pets are often necessary in wills drafted for LG clients. More states are recognizing the importance of pets in estate planning. Leaving an entire estate to a pet is unlikely to be honored in court; however, it is possible to provide for the care of a person's pets in a testamentary document, as discussed below.

It is important to discuss pets with the client when planning the estate. The issues include whether the person wants the pet euthanized when the surviving partner dies. Older pets may not be suitable for adoption or placement in a foster home. Often, the pets are overlooked in the overall estate plan, and this can be tragic for the animals involved.

While this situation is not unique to LG clients, it is advisable to cover the topic with the client in order to avoid a future dispute or misunderstanding.

Executor

In most situations, the executor will be the testator's partner. However, it may be necessary to discuss whether a professional entity (e.g., bank, trust company) would be better suited to administer the estate. This is particularly true with large estates where the tax consequences are potentially significant. Of course, if the estate is that large, planning is required to minimize the tax consequences.

While it may be possible to determine the amount of federal estate tax under the current circumstances, it may be impossible to determine the state tax liability. Many states traditionally based their estate tax on the federal tax table. That is rapidly changing given the recent steps taken by Congress to eliminate estate taxes.

State action can make estate planning more difficult because there may be no way to determine a legislature's future actions. Advising the client that the situation is currently in a state of flux can relieve the client's anxiety. The attorney, however, will need to monitor the situation and be prepared to advise all clients of changes that affect their estate plans.

The alternate executor must be someone who will support the surviving partner while administering the estate. The executor must be willing to follow the dictates of the testator, enforce her wishes, and dispose of the estate according to the terms of the will.

Appointment of a Guardian

A growing number of LG couples are starting families. Some adopt and others become biological parents.

Second-parent adoptions, where the nonbiological parent is the same sex, are not recognized or permitted in all states. Some states will not recognize a second-parent adoption granted in another state. This poses a legal conundrum for lesbian and gay clients that is not faced by heterosexual couples—even those who are not married.

Generally, when a parent dies, the surviving biological parent has superior rights to all others unless the parent is deemed unfit. In cases involving lesbian or gay parents, there is usually only one parent legally recognized by the state: the biological parent. The nonbiological surviving partner has no legal right.

However, nominating a person as guardian of the child in a will does present a rebuttable presumption of the deceased parent's preference. This will enhance the surviving partner's claim to be named the child's guardian.

It is also important to include the testator's reasons for selecting the person nominated as the guardian. Incorporating language that explains why family members were not named permits the testator to leave a written record of her reasons.

The biological parent can nominate the nonbiological parent to serve as the minor child's guardian, but the court is under no obligation to follow that suggestion. The court may appoint a member of the decedent's family as guardian, even if the surviving partner is the nominated guardian in the will. This can effectively terminate contact between the child and the surviving partner.

Second-parent adoptions may obviate the need for extensive drafting in the guardian clause. A court-sanctioned adoption lends legal validity to the nominated guardian's claim. At the very least, it raises the specter of a full-fledged court battle over who will be responsible for the child.

The testator is also able to name a guardian for the child's estate. This need not be the same as the guardian of the child's person. Therefore, the guardian clause may provide that the surviving partner will administer the child's estate. This allows the surviving partner to remain in the child's life and gives the child a sense of security.

A third section of the guardian clause is to include the naming of a person to serve as the child's interim guardian. If no one is named, the child may be placed in foster care until the courts resolve the issue of who will care for the child. The child might also be placed with a family member who is not the deceased parent's choice and with whom the child may not have had a prior relationship. Losing a parent is traumatic enough for a child. A child's best interests are not served by placing her in an unsettled home situation.

In matters involving children, it is difficult to provide for every scenario. It is, therefore, important to investigate all available options including the current status of second-parent adoptions in your jurisdiction. If it is allowed, or if the issue is undetermined, your client may want to pursue such an adoption.

A child is not entitled to any government benefits upon the death of the parent who is not legally related to the child. There are no survivor benefits for the child even if the decedent was the primary wage earner in the family. The child may also be unable to recoup benefits from the decedent's employer. For these reasons, second-parent adoption may provide the best protection for children of same-sex couples. This is particularly true in those states that do not recognize same-sex families. Children should be protected, not punished for the gender of their parents.

There may be an objection alleging that having the surviving partner in the child's life will be detrimental to the child. There is no guarantee that the court will honor the biological parent's wishes.

Trusts

Trusts comprise another facet of an estate plan for LG clients. In some ways trusts can provide the protection and privacy many clients seek. Trusts are usually more difficult for unhappy family members to contest. Trusts are not subject to the vagaries of probate court and are sometimes a better vehicle to protect the parties' intent.

It is important to remind clients that a will is necessary even if a trust is established. This is obvious where testamentary trusts are concerned. However, living trusts are also popular. When a living trust is used, a will can contain "pour-over" provisions that permit the testator to pass on assets that may have been left out of the trust. Without a will any nontrust assets pass under the state's intestate succession statute.

Some individuals with large estates may want to divest themselves of property during their lifetime. Section 2035(a) of the Internal Revenue Code deals with the transfer of a property interest within three years of death. The Internal Revenue Service considers that transfers made within that period are made in contemplation of death. The transfer is ignored and the value of that property must be included in the decedent's gross estate. This applies only to property that would be included in the decedent's gross estate under the IRC if the interest had been retained.

If the client funds an irrevocable life insurance trust with an existing policy and then dies within three years, the full value of the policy may be included in her gross estate. Such a result may have an adverse effect on the client's estate plan, especially if the insurance was intended to pay any estate taxes. It is important, therefore, to work with your clients to avoid unintended results.

Revocable trusts have no gift, income, or estate tax consequences. This is because the grantor retains control of the assets. The grantor continues to have the power to amend, revoke, or terminate the trust.

Irrevocable trusts, on the other hand, require that the grantor relinquish all rights to alter, amend, revoke, or terminate the trust. The grantor may retain certain administrative rights.

Living Trusts

Living trusts can be an appropriate vehicle to protect assets, maintain privacy, and avoid potentially negative family interaction when one of the partners dies.

There are two kinds of living trusts, revocable and irrevocable. In a revocable living trust, the grantor retains control over the administration and enforcement of the trust. In an irrevocable living trust, the grantor relinquishes all authority over the trust. The trust cannot be terminated nor can its provisions be changed. Once established, it remains in effect under the provisions of the trust and the supervision of the trustee.

A revocable living trust can be amended or revoked by the person creating the trust. The beneficiary of the trust cannot contest any action taken by the grantor. The grantor retains all the benefits of property placed into the trust. As with any other type of trust, its terms are spelled out in the trust document. This stipulates the duties and powers of the grantor and the trustee. The language also specifies what happens to the trust property during and after the grantor's life. The grantor and the trustee sign the trust. Often, the grantor is the trustee during his lifetime.

Most people use a living trust to avoid probate. Current probate practice is less intimidating than in the past. There are also other avenues available to people wishing to avoid probate that do not require the expense of establishing a living trust. As discussed in Chapter 5, these include payable-on-death accounts, transfer-on-death deeds, and joint accounts.

To avoid probate by creating a living trust, the grantor must transfer all property into the trust. This includes property owned at the time the trust is established and other property accumulated during the grantor's lifetime. Anything not placed into the trust is, potentially, a probate asset. Attorneys are well suited to advise the client on what property to transfer into the trust and to assist the client in effecting the transfer. Clients may also need an annual reminder to ensure they transfer recently acquired property into the trust.

These trusts can be used to meet the unique needs of a couple that has no statutory legal resource in the estate planning area. A living trust will give the parties privacy since the trust will never become a public record. The trust gives more control because the probate court is not involved. The trustee has considerable power and is not required to answer to anyone other than the grantor.

One significant advantage is the ability of the trustee to begin making distributions to the beneficiary soon after the grantor's death. In probate the distribution can take months.

Another advantage involves real estate that is owned in different states. Unlike a probate case, there is no need for an ancillary proceeding when the property is held in trust. Since many LG individuals and couples own property in different states, this is a reason to discuss a living trust with the client.

It is wise to point out that a living trust provides a significant benefit to the grantor if she becomes incompetent during her lifetime. Without a trust it would be necessary to initiate a guardianship proceeding. This can be time-consuming, expensive, and frustrating. A guardianship proceeding also allows a probate court to find that a family member is in a better position to care for the incompetent person than the gay or lesbian partner.

Sharon Kowalski is a well-known example of a guardianship contest. Her partner ultimately prevailed over Ms. Kowalski's parents, but it took years of court battles and many thousands of dollars in attorney fees and court costs. Also, during that time Ms. Kowalski had virtually no contact with her long-time partner because her parents would not allow it.

Ms. Kowalski became completely disabled following a 1983 automobile accident. At the time of the accident she shared a home with her partner, Karen Thompson. Ms. Kowalski's parents were unaware of her lesbian relationship. The guardianship battle began in 1984 when Ms. Thompson and Ms. Kowalski's father cross-petitioned for guardianship. Ms. Thompson agreed to the father's appointment as guardian. She fully expected to be able to visit and have input on Ms. Kowalski's medical care decisions. The guardianship order, however, gave full authority over visitation to Mr. Kowalski and he, with the court's approval, terminated Ms. Thompson's visitation rights in 1985.

Three years later another court reinstated Ms. Thompson's visitation rights. In 1988 Ms. Thompson again applied to be appointed Ms. Kowalski's guardian. In spite of substantial evidence supporting her petition, the court appointed a friend of Ms. Kowalski's family to be the guardian. Ms. Thompson appealed to the Minnesota Court of Appeals. That court reversed the case and remanded with instructions to appoint Ms. Thompson as Ms. Kowalski's guardian. The case took eight years to resolve.[2]

Living trusts provide LG clients an avenue to protect their assets and their relationship from inquiry by courts and the public. The trust can hold both shared and individually held property. This makes the setup and administration easier.

Clients need to be aware that creditors can access assets in a revocable living trust. Irrevocable living trusts are different. A bona fide irrevocable living trust precludes creditors from attaching any assets because the grantor relinquishes all authority of administration and enforcement of the trust.

Clients also need to understand that a living trust, while avoiding probate, does not necessarily avoid potential liability for estate or death taxes. Too many people believe they do not have to pay taxes if they have a living trust. This is incorrect and it is important that the client understands that fact.

---

2. Guardianship of Kowalski, 478 N.W.2d 790 (Minn. Ct. App., Dec. 17, 1991).

The assets placed in a living trust, revocable or irrevocable, constitute a decedent's estate. Probate does not control a decedent's taxable estate. Non-probate assets can still remain part of a decedent's estate and, therefore, subject to estate taxes.

For example, if the assets in a living trust are valued in excess of $1 million, federal estate tax will be due on the amount that exceeds the current floor. In 2003, the estate tax floor was $1 million. This amount will go up over the next several years until it is repealed in 2010. However, in 2011, the estate tax is scheduled to be reinstated at the $1 million level.

A living trust, in and of itself, is not a tax-planning tool. Clients with large estates must consult a tax planner to take advantage of all available tax credits and exemptions. This is done to reduce the amount of a person's taxable estate.

In addition to federal estate tax, the assets in a living trust may also be subject to state estate taxes. This is also a consideration when drafting the trust documents.

Testamentary Trusts

Testamentary trusts are the more traditional type used in estate plans. Using trusts can provide tax benefits for the clients. However, it is very important to protect against conflict of interest when representing both parties in designing an estate plan. Having the parties sign an "acknowledgement of representation" can neutralize this. In this document you set forth the situation and advise both parties that nothing will be kept from the other. If that creates a problem, you may wish to consider withdrawing or representing only one client. (See Appendix A for a sample letter.)

It is not unusual for one partner to have a higher income than the other. One partner may own the property or the business while the other stays at home caring for the household and the children. The potential ramifications of this arrangement may not have occurred to either partner.

A disadvantage of a testamentary trust is that the assets must usually go through probate. A testamentary trust does not come into effect until the death of the trustor. That is the significant difference between this and the *inter vivos* trust.

Spendthrift Trusts

Lesbian and gay clients can consider several types of testamentary trusts. If one partner has a significant estate and is concerned about her partner squandering the wealth, a spendthrift trust may be considered.

A spendthrift trust prevents a beneficiary from squandering the trust principal. The beneficiary is never the trustee, but the trustee can make payments directly to the beneficiary. The beneficiary has no right to spend the trust principal or encumber the trust in any way. This trust also prevents the beneficiary's creditors from gaining access to the principal.

A spendthrift trust can also provide that the trustee is not authorized to make direct cash payments to the beneficiary. The trust can authorize the trustee to make payments directly to a provider of services such as a landlord or utility company.

This type of testamentary trust can be as rigid or flexible as the trustor deems appropriate. But it is important not to create a trust that is so burdensome on the trustee that no one wants to serve in that capacity. It is also important to determine when and how the trust will be terminated and what happens to the trust principal when termination occurs.

A spendthrift provision can be included in any trust. It is a restraint on the voluntary or involuntary alienation of a beneficiary's interest in a trust. The clause provides that the beneficiary shall neither transfer nor assign the interest. Likewise, the beneficiary's interest is not subject to creditor's claims. A sample provision may be

> No beneficiary shall have the right to transfer all or part of his interest either in income or principal unless the Trustee, in its discretion, shall consent in writing. The Trustee shall not be compelled to exercise this discretion. No person, having a claim or demand of any sort against the beneficiary, shall have the right to reach the interest of any beneficiary by judicial process while the Trustee has possession of any trust assets.

Most states will not enforce a spendthrift clause where the grantor and the beneficiary are the same person. However, some states will enforce such clauses when the same person wears both hats. It is, therefore, necessary to check your state law.

Discretionary Trusts

A discretionary or "special needs" trust is another type of testamentary trust that should be discussed with any gay or lesbian couple. This is particularly true if either partner is ill. In the gay community it is not unheard of for one or both partners to be suffering from AIDS or be HIV-positive. A discretionary or special needs trust may serve the purpose of providing for the surviving partner on the death of the other.

A discretionary trust gives the trustee the choice of distributing the proceeds to a designated group of beneficiaries. There is no specification concerning what property each beneficiary receives or when. The trust authorizes the trustee to make all decisions concerning the distribution. The trustor specifies, in the trust document, when the trust will terminate and what happens to the trust res at that time. The alternative is to leave that determination to the discretion of the trustee.

In a situation where one partner is ill, it is advisable to limit the trustee's discretion to only pay medical bills that are not covered by a government benefits program (e.g., Medicaid or Medicare). And, the trust should prohibit the trustee from making cash payments directly to the beneficiary. This will limit, if not eliminate, any adverse impact on the beneficiary's receipt of public benefits (e.g., Supplemental Security Income).

The trustee named must be a disinterested trustee. The person named cannot have a financial interest in the trust, now or in the future.

Special needs trusts are authorized by the Omnibus Budget Reconciliation Act of 1993. This trust is also known as a Medicaid payback trust because it requires the trust to pay back an amount equal to what the state spent in providing the beneficiary with medical care. In this statute a "special needs trust" is defined as

> A trust containing the assets of an individual under age 65 who is disabled (as described in § 1382c(a)(3) of this title) and which is established for the benefit of such individual by a parent, grandparent, legal guardian of the individual or a court if the state will receive all amounts remaining in the trust upon the death of such individual up to an amount equal to the total medical assistance paid on behalf of the individual under a State plan under this subchapter.[3]

Note that only a member of a specific class of people may establish the trust. If one partner is named the legal guardian of the other, then a special needs trust can be established. The drafting requirements for this type of trust are stringent and must be carefully followed. However, it can provide additional resources to a disabled surviving partner for items that are not covered by Medicaid.

Many states define "supplemental services" that can be covered. This includes in-home nursing care or assistance. Most people want to stay home

---

3. 42 U.S.C. § 1396p(d)(4)(A).

as long as possible. This type of trust may allow a disabled surviving partner to do just that.

Pet Trusts[1]

Testamentary trusts are another possibility for pet owners to consider in providing for their pets. Thirteen states have laws permitting people to establish trusts that name pets as beneficiaries. These laws provide that a trust can be established and enforced by a person acting on behalf of the animal.

In states that do not have pet trust statutes, lawyers are drafting trusts that indirectly benefit the companion animals. These trusts name a caretaker beneficiary and stipulate that the beneficiary receives distributions only if the pet is being cared for properly. The trustee of these trusts is responsible for ensuring the pet's care; therefore, it is important that the trustee and caretaker beneficiary are not the same person.

The trusts work for people concerned about the care of their pets who do not want to leave the pet and a sum of money to an individual outright.

The amount left in trust will depend on a number of factors including the type of animal, age and health of the animal, and the type of care the owner wishes to provide. For example, a horse will require a greater amount than a gerbil.

A trust can also include specific property items such as a house or vehicle to be used by the beneficiary for the benefit of the animal. The trust can then provide for the disposition of this property upon the death of the animal and the trust's termination.

Trusts that are established with the pet as the beneficiary are risky if there is no pet trust statute. Courts are not inclined to find them valid for a number of reasons, including violating the rule against perpetuities. This is because some pets live longer than twenty-one years.

The Uniform Probate Code, amended in 1993 to address this situation, seems to solve the problem. According to Section 2-907, a trust for the care of a pet or companion animal is valid and can continue until the animal's death. "An individual designated for that purpose in the trust instrument" can enforce this trust. If no one is designated, the court can appoint someone when an application is filed. The court can reduce the amount designated to fund the trust if the judge finds that amount to be excessive.

---

1. *Trusts to Care for Pets after Death Catching On*, James L. Dam., LAWYERS WEEKLY USA, July 22, 2002, available at http://www.lawyersweeklyusa.com/reprints/pettrusts.htm.

Most of the states that have this type of trust include similar provisions. For example, the Colorado law provides that a trust can continue until the pet's offspring that were in gestation at the time of the owner's death die. New York and New Jersey, on the other hand, limit the trust length to twenty-one years.

The pet trust statutes treat this trust in a manner similar to that for a minor child. The person appointed to enforce the trust is in a position comparable to that of a guardian.

A trustor need only name a class of animals and provide the funds. There is no need to name each animal individually. The client should also name a trustee, a caretaker, and an enforcer, if different from the trustee, and alternates to each. It is best to ensure that these people will follow the trustor's instructions and intent.

The trust must also include the provisions or guidelines the trustor wants to establish for the pet's care: annual or monthly expenditure expectations and the procedures for paying them, type of food, and payment of caretaker's fee, veterinary fees, and pet health care insurance premiums. These same details may be included in a separate document, but including them in the trust language gives them greater emphasis.

The trustor may also want to stipulate how major decisions concerning the pet are to be made. This would include if and when to euthanize the animal. The trust can provide that such decisions are to be made by a panel of designated people.

Another form of trust is to name the caretaker as the beneficiary. Then the caretaker can enforce the trust by demanding payment for services provided. An alternative is to allow the trustee to enforce the trust by withholding payments or replacing the caretaker if proper care is not provided. Alternate caretakers can provide another form of enforcement by demanding proper care for the pet and, if not given, to demand that the caretaker be replaced.

This type of trust can last for the life of the caretaker plus twenty-one years or terminate when the pet dies, whichever comes first. Of course, the trust may provide for the event that the pet outlives the caretaker and the twenty-one years.

One problem with this type of caretaker/beneficiary trust arises when no one named in the trust wants to assume the responsibilities involved. If this situation is a possibility, the trustor may want to name an organization rather than an individual. There are a growing number of groups that are establishing homes to which pet owners can send their animals for lifelong care.

One example of this is the Bide-A-Wee Golden Years Retirement Home in Westhampton, New York (http://www.bideawee.org). The animals they accept must be at least eight years old and the charge is $10,000.

Other options for concerned pet owners are no-kill shelters or pet retirement homes. The best known, nationally recognized no-kill facility is Best Friends in Kanab, Utah (http://www.bestfriends.org). Pet Estates in Albany, New York is a pet retirement home. There is no golf course at Pet Estates but they do offer lifetime care for pets. The cost for this care runs from $7,300 to $21,400, depending on the services requested. Clients provide for Pet Estates in the will or trust.

Generally, dogs cost more than cats. The annual cost for a dog ranges from $780 to $1500, while a cat runs an average of $640.

Organizations that qualifiy as 501(c)(3) nonprofit entities may be provided for in a charitable trust. This can assist the client in any necessary tax planning and provides another topic for discussion.

The Humane Society of the United States has a free estate-planning kit for pets (http://www.hsus.org/petsinwills).

In states that do not have pet trust statutes, there is a real danger that a court will deem any pet trust invalid because the pet is seen as the real beneficiary. To get around this, the trust can provide that the trustee is to make direct payments for medical care and annual payments to the caretaker so long as the pet is being cared for properly.

The trust can also provide for payments to the caretaker for a set period of years. After that time ownership of the pet is transferred to the caretaker and the trust is terminated. The balance of the trust res can be paid out to the caretaker when the trust terminates.

In any event, the care and feeding of companion animals is something that must be discussed with any LG clients.

Charitable Remainder Trusts

In some cases the lesbian or gay client may have a significant estate that renders it potentially liable for estate taxes. In that case the client may wish to consider creating an irrevocable charitable remainder trust. This trust allows the client to make a gift to a charity of choice and also name someone to receive the income from the donated property.

The property can be donated during the grantor's lifetime. The trust makes a series of specific payments, defined in the trust document, to the income beneficiary. The beneficiary can be the grantor and her partner, or anyone else named by the grantor. Payments can be a percentage of the gift's value or a specific amount. The payments can run for a set period of time or the beneficiary can be given a life estate interest in the payments.

When the donated property is real estate, a donor may make the donation during his lifetime and retain a life estate for himself. That gives the donor the right to retain the use of the property during his lifetime with the charity receiving clear title upon his death. The donor may specify who is responsible for upkeep and taxes during his lifetime.

There are various benefits to this type of trust. These include an income tax deduction for the trust's creator and a reduced estate tax liability since the value of the donated property is removed from the grantor's estate. The charity benefits from any increase in the property's appreciated value.

There are two types of charitable remainder trusts: charitable remainder annuity trusts and charitable remainder unitrusts. They are defined in Sections 664(d) and 664(a), respectively, of the Internal Revenue Code. The IRS has also issued sample charitable trust forms. Revenue Procedure 90-30 contains five sample forms of Section 664(d)(2) *inter vivos* and testamentary charitable remainder unitrusts for two lives with consecutive interests and two lives with concurrent and consecutive interests. It also contains a testamentary trust for one life. Revenue Procedure 89-20 contains a sample form for an *inter vivos* charitable remainder trust with one measuring life. Revenue Procedure 90-31 provides six samples of Sections 664(d)(2) and (3) charitable remainder unitrusts for *inter vivos* and testamentary trusts for one life, two lives with consecutive interests, and two lives with concurrent and consecutive interests. Revenue Procedure 90-32 presents five sample forms of the Section 664(d)(1) *inter vivos* and testamentary charitable remainder annuity trusts for two lives with consecutive interests and two lives with concurrent and consecutive interests. It also provides a sample testamentary trust for one life. Revenue Procedure 89-21 contains a sample form for an *inter vivos* charitable remainder trust with one measuring life.[4]

These forms may assist you in developing an appropriate charitable remainder trust for your clients.

Irrevocable Life Insurance Trusts

An irrevocable life insurance trust provides the client with an opportunity to buy an insurance policy but remove it from the taxable estate. This trust is

---

4. Rev. Proc. 90-30, 1990-1 C.B. 534; Rev. Proc. 89-20, 1989-1 C.B. 841; Rev. Proc. 90-31, 1990-1 C.B. 539; Rev. Proc. 90-32, 1990-1 C.B. 546; Rev. Proc. 89-21, 1989-1 C.B. 842.

established during the life of the policyholder. All incidents of ownership are given to the trust. Once transferred, the trust owns the policy and has complete control over its administration.

There are requirements for a valid life insurance trust. The trust must be irrevocable. Any retention of rights will invalidate the trust for tax purposes. The owner of the policy cannot be the trustee. If the grantor owned the policy, the trust must be established at least three years before the grantor's death. Otherwise, the trust will be discarded and the proceeds included in the taxable estate.

Taxes

Under current federal law each person with an estate of $1 million or less will not incur any federal estate tax liability. This amount gradually increases to $3.5 million in 2009. The federal estate tax is scheduled to be repealed in 2010 and reinstated at the $1 million level in 2011, unless Congress decides to make the repeal permanent.

Application of the tax laws does not depend on the taxpayer's sexual orientation. Every individual lesbian or gay client can take advantage of these tax laws. Married heterosexual couples may transfer between themselves an unlimited amount of assets under the marital exemption. There is no marital exemption for lesbian and gay couples.

There are ways that a same-sex couple can maximize the tax laws on their individual returns. LG couples need to consider tax issues involving jointly held property, children or other dependents, and shared income, including business income.

Lesbian and gay couples must file as single taxpayers. They cannot file a joint federal tax return. There is no exception to this restriction. The Defense of Marriage Act states that no federal law applies to same-sex couples.

LG clients should consider various methods of filing their tax returns. Clients can compile all deductions and determine which partner will benefit more from itemizing. One exception is the home mortgage. Only the person responsible for the mortgage can deduct the interest. However, where the property is jointly held and both partners are on the mortgage, either can take the full deduction.

Transferring ownership of income-producing assets to the partner with the lower income may also provide aggregate tax relief. It is important, however, to consider any gift tax consequences of such a transfer. Of course, clients need to execute a written agreement before making the transfer. This is particularly true if real property is involved.

Clients should remember to consider dependents, deductions, and distribution when calculating tax liability. For example, a stay-at-home partner supported by the working partner may qualify as a dependent. The working partner may also qualify as a head of household.

Educational and medical payments can also be made by one partner on behalf of the other and claimed as a deduction. There is no restriction on the amount of medical and educational payments as long as they are made directly to the health care provider or the educational institution.

A taxpayer's medical expenses must exceed 7.5 percent of adjusted gross income in order to itemize. Consider advising that one partner pay for both parties' medical expenses until the threshold is reached. For example, have one person pay for all medicines. Also, if one of the partners is self-employed, he can deduct 100 percent of his health care premiums. If he has a family plan that includes his partner, that can result in significant savings at tax time.

Couples who have a joint account, and pay all bills from that account, may want to consider individual accounts for tax purposes. Detailed records concerning the source of the money used is important to withstand any IRS audit.

Gift Taxes

Gift tax issues arise in gay relationships usually because one partner transfers property into both names. This typically happens with real estate. Often one partner owns a house when the relationship begins. At some point, they decide to own the property jointly. This transfer triggers a gift tax scenario.

Under federal tax law, every person has a lifetime gift tax exemption of $1 million. This means that, over the course of a lifetime, each one of us can give away up to $1 million in assets without paying any taxes.

Every person has the right to make an annual gift up to $11,000 to anyone. There is no limit on the number of $11,000 gifts one person can make in any given year. These annual gifts do *not* count against the $1 million exemption amount.

Gifts that exceed the $11,000 amount must be reported on the federal gift tax return by April 15 of the year following the gift. The amount over $11,000 is deducted from the lifetime exemption amount of $1 million. As long as the gifts stay below the $11,000 annual limit, there is no need to file a gift tax return.

Most LG couples do not consider the gift tax aspect of a transfer. The gift tax issue arises because there is a divestiture of interest from one party to the other. Both now own a one-half interest in the property.

There is no gift tax liability for amounts paid on medical and educational expenses. Payments for medical and educational expenses for another are not governed by the $11,000 annual maximum. The only requirement is that the payments must be made directly to the provider or institution.

The important feature of this gift tax exclusion is that it is available without regard to the relationship between the parties. One partner can pay tuition directly to a college for the other partner. There is no gift tax liability because it is not part of the $1 million lifetime exemption.

Likewise, if one partner is ill the other partner can pay the health care provider directly for services rendered. This exclusion can be very beneficial in tax planning for a gay or lesbian client who itemizes.

Jointly Held Property

Even if property is held in joint tenancy with rights of survivorship, there remains an estate tax issue for unmarried couples. The IRS includes the entire value of the property in the estate of the first owner to die unless the surviving joint owner can provide evidence of her contribution to the acquisition of the property. Without evidence establishing the contribution made by the surviving partner, the entire value of the property is also included in the estate of the second owner when she dies. In effect, the property is being taxed twice.

Married couples do not face this double taxation penalty. The IRS presumes that husband and wife holding jointly titled property own equal shares.

IRAs

The full value of a qualified retirement plan or IRA is included in the estate of the first partner to die. The IRA then becomes a "beneficiary IRA" and the beneficiary has two choices: begin regular distributions over the life of the beneficiary or withdraw everything by the end of the fifth year following the original owner's death. These distributions are taxable to the surviving partner-beneficiary when they are received.

Again, this is dramatically different from the situation faced by a married couple. In that case, the surviving spouse can roll over the assets and defer distribution until age seventy. This allows the distribution to continue to grow tax-free. This option is not available to same-sex couples.

State Death Taxes

The effect of the changes in federal estate taxes on state estate taxes is yet to be determined. Most states that have a state "death" tax are piggybacked onto the federal estate tax formula, under a so-called pick-up tax. This is an arrangement between the states and the federal government. There is nothing an individual can do about it.

This arrangement, however, is changing because of the changes in the federal estate tax. Some states are now calculating estate taxes independently of the federal government. It is impossible to say how this will come out in the end.

One-third of the states changed their laws in order to decouple the state death tax from the federal estate tax. Some states include estates of less than $1 million when calculating state estate taxes. Example: New Jersey, Rhode Island, and Wisconsin tax estates starting at $675,000. Oregon starts at $700,000. Ohio and Oklahoma tax the whole estate. Ohio grants an exemption of $338,333 after which the tax is 6 percent or 7 percent.

Eighteen states and the District of Columbia changed their laws to keep estate taxes coming into state coffers. These states are demanding the same amount of death taxes to which they were entitled under the old rules. In these states a decedent's estates will pay more in death taxes than in other states. The states are Illinois, Kansas, Maine, Maryland, Massachusetts, Minnesota, Nebraska, New Jersey, New York, North Carolina, Ohio, Oregon, Pennsylvania, Rhode Island, Vermont, Virginia, Washington, and Wisconsin. The rest are letting the pick-up tax fade away. The estimated cost to those states is $15 billion from 2003 to 2007.[5]

Thirteen states levy death taxes. These are Connecticut, Indiana, Iowa, Kentucky, Louisiana, Maryland, Nebraska, New Hampshire, New Jersey, Ohio, Oklahoma, Pennsylvania, and Tennessee. Louisiana and Connecticut are phasing their death taxes out by 2004 and 2005, respectively. Nebraska has only a county inheritance tax.

If your client lives in one of the death tax states, there may be a penalty involved with leaving property to someone who is not considered "legal family." States provide classes of death tax exemptions. The percentage allowed for the exemption depends on the legal relationship with the decedent. Surviving spouses, for example, have a 100 percent exemption. This is in keeping with the federal estate tax marital deduction.

Once you get past the surviving spouse, however, the situation can change dramatically. The lowest exemption allowance is for "strangers," those beneficiaries who have no legal relationship with the decedent.

For example, in Indiana, Class A includes spouse, parents, children, and grandchildren; Class B includes siblings, nieces, nephews, and sons/daughters-

---

5. Center on Budget and Policy Priorities.

in-law; and Class C includes all others. The percentage depends on the amount of the estate. The range for Class A is a base tax plus 0 percent to base tax plus 10 percent. Class C starts at base tax plus 10 percent and rises to base tax plus 20 percent.

A gay or lesbian partner falls into the Class C category. It is important, therefore, to check the state laws where your client holds property to determine the effect of the death tax on that client.

The estate tax issue is in a state of flux. No one can predict what the outcome will be on the federal, state, or even the local level. It is important, therefore, to advise clients of the uncertainties. Avoiding taxes may not be within the exclusive provenance of LG clients, but given the care these clients take in preparing their estate, it is an important concern.

Other Considerations

Clients should be advised to include a letter of instruction for their executor and survivors. This letter is an informal document that gives specific instructions that cannot be altered. The client can leave the letter with the executor. The alternative is to provide the executor with information concerning the whereabouts of the letter. This letter would include the following information:

- Client's name (including aliases), address, date of birth, place of birth, citizenship status, Social Security number
- Partner's name, contact information, date of birth, place of birth, citizenship status, Social Security number
- Names, contact information, dates of birth, places of birth for all children
- Information on armed forces service, including date of discharge and location of discharge papers (DD-214)
- Address of employer with human resource contact information
- Names and contact information for everyone the client wants notified upon death
- Location of key documents, including the will
- Funeral and burial instructions, even if included in the designation of agent form
- Personal matters not included in the will, but helpful to the executor: location of bank accounts and numbers; location of insurance policy and policy numbers; brokerage accounts (type); names and contact

numbers for broker, banker, and insurance agent; names of beneficiaries on each account or policy; credit card accounts (include location
of all cards) and contact information for credit card companies; location of deeds; location of safe deposit box or home safe and how to
get into it; names of all who have access to safe deposit box or home
safe; description of death benefits due; list of assets (personal and real
estate); emotional maturity of any children; description of relationship with family members

- Instructions for what to include in the obituary; biographical information including major employers, honors received, education, membership in professional organizations, and notable achievements
- Inscription to be placed on the headstone or grave surface

Conclusion

Creating an estate plan for your LG clients requires that you consider
issues not usually apparent or applicable in heterosexual estates. You are in
a position to guide your clients through the process and remind them to consider matters they may not otherwise think about. Preparing an extensive and
comprehensive will questionnaire for the clients to complete is a good way to
start the process. The questionnaire serves as the means to prod clients into
thinking about the entire process and not just the obvious.

Chapter 5

Avoiding Probate

Most people want to avoid probate because of the perceived cost and time involved. There is also the belief that avoiding probate increases the control the individual has over her estate after death.

Lesbian and gay clients are interested in establishing an estate plan that will provide protection for their designated beneficiaries and prevent challenges from estranged or vindictive family members. Avoiding probate takes on even greater importance when a partner is faced with the prospect of losing everything simply because someone does not like the gender of the person with whom one sleeps.

There are times, however, when probate is preferable. The probate court provides supervision and procedures that are unavailable in a nonprobate situation. This can prove useful because it is possible to take advantage of the laws that govern the probate process. For example, challenges must be filed within a defined period of time and accountings are required on a regular basis. The rules are clearly set forth in statutes and apply evenly to all parties. These procedures also help executors fend off will challenges by someone unhappy with the document's provisions.

Probate can also be helpful if the estate has a large amount of debt. Creditors are required to submit claims within a specified period of time. Failure to meet those requirements will leave a procrastinating creditor in the dust. The executor is then able to close the estate and distribute the assets according to the testator's wishes.

Without probate the decedent's assets remain subject to any outstanding debts. Probate also does nothing to alleviate or minimize any estate taxes. The beneficiaries of the testator's largess need to be reminded that the estate property will be used to pay off debts. Beneficiaries under a will receive the residue of the estate after payment of debts and expenses.

Standard Methods of Avoiding Probate

Avoiding probate is not that difficult but does require advance planning. Living trusts, joint tenancy, payable-on-death accounts, transfer-on-death provisions, life insurance, pension or retirement fund designations, and *inter vivos* gifts are some of the ways to avoid probate. Some of these formats are easy to create and administer; others require more time, effort and money.

Living Trusts

Living trusts, discussed in the previous chapter, are among the most popular ways, and sometimes the most obvious way, to avoid probate. As discussed previously, a living, or *inter vivos,* trust can be either revocable or irrevocable.

A revocable living trust gives the grantor complete control over her property during her lifetime. These trusts also provide a flexible format in which to make changes to asset distribution and for management of those assets in times of incapacity.

Living trusts are, however, more expensive to set up than the average will. They also can be more expensive to administer both during the grantor's life and after her death. And, there is the matter of funding the trust once it is established.

The client must be told about the need to fund the trust. Clients often believe that once they sign the document the trust exists automatically. They do not know about taking the necessary steps to transfer their assets into the trust. Should the client fail to properly fund, her efforts to protect assets will be futile.

In order to avoid this calamitous result, the attorney may take on the task of retitling assets into the trust. This increases the cost of preparing the living trust but it does ensure that the trust is properly funded. It is a service to offer a client and one that can be handled by an attorney's support staff.

Some attorneys send their clients annual written reminders to make sure that any assets accumulated during the year have been properly titled as part of the trust res. This is a good client service. This type of practice also minimizes the possibility of a viable malpractice claim.

Joint Tenancy

Joint tenancy is a form of property ownership. Its primary use is for real estate. Its main benefit is the "right of survivorship" provision. When one joint tenant dies the surviving joint tenant takes sole ownership of the property.

Joint tenancy is perhaps the best way to avoid probate where real estate is involved. By jointly titling all property, with right of survivorship, the owners guarantee that the property will pass to the survivor and outside the probate process. Another advantage is that this format is not subject to challenge.

There can be multiple joint tenants but this is inadvisable for several reasons. The property will become subject to the debts of each individual joint owner. Further, an individual owner may sell his share to another party. That action destroys the survivorship provisions and makes all owners tenants in common. This form of ownership is disposed of by will or, if the tenant dies without a will, by the state law of intestate succession. Joint tenancy must be entered into carefully because of these and other drawbacks. It is important to discuss the advantages and disadvantages with your clients.

Each joint tenant will have an equal share. Unequal shares cannot usually be sustained in a joint tenancy; however, it is important to review the law in your jurisdiction.

Some states, including Alaska, allow only married couples to enter into an "estate by the entireties." There is no other statutory provision for joint ownership of real estate in Alaska.

Joint tenancy works very well with two people. Each then holds a 50 percent share of the property. The surviving joint tenant receives the decedent's 50 percent and thereby gains sole control over the property.

It is a good idea for the will to mention how specific property is titled. This clarifies the status of the property. When the property is sold or transferred, the will must be rewritten to reflect that change.

Any provision of the will that attempts to dispose of property held in joint tenancy will be ignored. A will cannot be used to overcome a joint tenancy designation on a recorded deed.

Even if a home is held in joint tenancy, lesbians and gay men do not receive the exemption from property tax reassessment when the other owner dies. This is also true in cases where the property title is transferred by will.

The Internal Revenue Service presumes that the first person to die owned 100 percent of the property. The survivor must provide documentation showing his contributions to the purchase and upkeep of the home. This includes receipts and tax returns for the years in which the couple jointly owned the property.

Another consideration is that the transfer of title from joint tenancy to a single owner is a change of ownership for property tax purposes. This transfer may result in a reassessment of property taxes. That reassessment may result in the surviving partner being forced to sell the property in order to pay the taxes. This is where a life insurance policy may become necessary. The life insurance will provide a liquid asset that the surviving partner can use to pay any property tax increase.

Joint tenancy is not limited to real estate. People can open bank accounts as joint tenants. Both parties have equal rights in and access to the account. Joint tenancy accounts can include checking, savings, certificate of deposit, and other common bank accounts. All tenants sign the required bank form as "joint tenants with right of survivorship."

These accounts require only one signature as both joint tenants have equal access to the funds. However, it is possible for the joint tenants to arrange with the bank that two signatures are required for any withdrawal.

Creation of a joint tenancy in a bank account creates an immediate and present interest in both parties to the account assets. However, no gift results from setting up a joint tenancy account.

Gift taxes come into play in another way. If one joint tenant is making all the deposits, a gift is made whenever the other tenant withdraws money. As long as the total amount, on a yearly basis, is $11,000 or less, there is no gift tax liability. It is important for both parties to a joint tenancy account to keep detailed and accurate records concerning deposits to the account.

In any joint tenancy, whether bank accounts or real estate, the assets will be included in the estate of the first joint tenant to die. If the surviving joint tenant cannot establish, to the satisfaction of the IRS, the amount of her contribution, the entire amount will be included in the decedent's taxable estate. With real estate, this includes any capital improvements. When the surviving tenant dies, the full amount of the account will be included in that estate. This can result in double taxation. Internal Revenue Code Section 2040 is the controlling section.

There is another tax pitfall involved with joint tenancies that lesbian and gay clients need to know. Example: One partner owns the house when the couple enters the relationship. After a period of time, the parties decide they want the house held in both names as joint tenants with rights of survivorship.

According to the IRS, a taxable gift is made when a joint tenancy is created and both partners did not make an equal contribution to the purchase of the property. In the above example, the parties merely added the second partner's name to the deed. The legal gift is one-half the ownership of the property. If the value exceeds $11,000, a federal gift tax return is required. The gift tax need not be paid at the time of filing. The assessed tax is deducted from the giftor's lifetime exemption of $1 million.

Another issue arises with incapacity. If one joint tenant becomes incapacitated, it may be difficult or impossible for the other joint tenant to sell, encumber, or otherwise dispose of the property. One way to avoid this is for both joint tenants to execute a durable power of attorney for finances. The alternative is for the competent tenant to petition the probate court to appoint a guardian.

Payable-on-Death Accounts

Payable-on-death (POD) accounts, also known as Totten trusts, permit the account holder to name a beneficiary of the account. The beneficiary receives all money in the account when the holder dies but has no present interest during the life of the account holder. The bank distributes the property directly to the named beneficiary without going through probate.

The client can check with the bank about the procedures the beneficiary must follow to obtain possession of the money. Some bank personnel believe a court order is required to release the account assets. State law and local court practice may determine what is required to obtain the release of assets from a POD account.

The account holder has full control over the account during her lifetime. The beneficiary has no present interest in, and no authority to access, the account during the holder's lifetime. There is no real downside to creating a POD account. Most financial institutions have standard forms used to name the beneficiary. There is usually no special procedure needed to establish a POD account.

The account holder can name multiple beneficiaries on a POD account. Each beneficiary receives an equal share of the account assets. Alternate beneficiaries cannot be provided for in a POD account. If the account holder is concerned that a named beneficiary will not outlive him then a POD account may be inappropriate.

When a named beneficiary predeceases the account holder and a new beneficiary is not named, the account proceeds are paid into the decedent's estate. This can create a probate asset.

POD accounts are a good way for gay and lesbian clients to provide for their partners. Many couples have joint bank accounts. However, some may retain separate accounts for any number of reasons. The POD account gives the gay client an opportunity to avoid probate and its potential for challenge to the holder's disposition of assets. Family members cannot dispute a POD designation.

The money in a POD account is included in the holder's taxable estate. This type of account carries no tax planning benefit, unless the beneficiary is a charity.

Government securities such as T-bills can also carry a POD designation. However, on these holdings there can be only one owner and one beneficiary.

More than one person can hold U.S. Savings Bonds as joint tenants. The forms for purchasing the bonds, generally Series E, can be found on the Federal Reserve Bank's Web site, http://www.frb.gov. The site also contains the forms and information for cashing in the bonds.

Savings bonds do not seem to hold the allure they once did, but are still held by many people. Some people have them from childhood when they received them as gifts. The client can name a partner as the joint tenant of the savings bond. If there is no designation, the bonds are included in the probate estate.

Payable-on-death securities accounts are another way to transfer assets outside of probate. Some states designate these as "Transfer on Death" accounts. Most brokerage firms have the necessary forms.

The client can designate individual stocks or brokerage accounts to be transferred upon death to a named beneficiary. This takes place under the Uniform Transfers-on-Death Securities Regulation Act.

Not all states permit a transfer-on-death of securities. In those that do, the securities or brokerage account assets are transferred promptly to the named beneficiary. There are four states that currently do not permit transfer-on-death registration: Louisiana, New York, North Carolina, and Texas. The District of Columbia does permit the registration.

Even if the client lives in a state that does not recognize TOD registration, it is still possible to accomplish this if the brokerage's principal office is in a state that does permit registration. This also holds true if the stock issuer is incorporated in a state that allows registration or if the transfer agent's office is in such a state.

When none of these opportunities present themselves, and the client is prevented from registering for a TOD designation, it may be appropriate to create a living trust. The goal of gay and lesbian clients is to ensure that their assets go where they want and are not subject to the vagaries of state inheritance laws. Plus, a living trust is better than joint tenancy in that the beneficiary will not enjoy a present interest in the asset. The grantor retains complete control over the asset until his death.

The securities, bonds, and other TOD holdings are transferred to the beneficiary upon the death of the holder. These are not considered to be probate assets.

Life Insurance

Life insurance is another method used to avoid probate. Insurance proceeds are paid directly to the named beneficiary, thereby bypassing probate. The only way life insurance proceeds are subject to probate jurisdiction is when the estate is the named beneficiary. There are very few reasons to name the estate as the beneficiary. An example is in the case of a large estate that has no liquid assets to pay taxes or costs.

Life insurance is included in the decedent's estate for tax purposes. Estate taxes are paid on the net estate. This results after all appropriate deductions are made. Estate taxes are levied on probate and nonprobate assets.

The federal estate tax is a situation that is changing on a regular basis. In 2004, there is a $1.5 million exemption from estate taxes.

Life insurance can be a factor in making an estate liable for taxes. A large insurance policy can make the overall estate subject to estate taxes. It is important, therefore, to determine the insurance status of the client when making estate plan recommendations. Many gay or lesbian clients who work with a financial planner have life insurance as part of their overall financial plan. Some of these policies can be significant.

The attorney may also suggest that clients consult a planner to determine if life insurance should be part of their overall estate plan.

Life insurance is included in an estate if the decedent owned the policy for the three years immediately preceding death. This includes paying the premiums and exercising control over the policy. Life insurance that is transferred within three years of death falls into the "contemplation of death" category for the IRS.

The agency seeks to identify the person who retained significant power over the policy. The agency's purpose, of course, is to determine if the policy proceeds are to be included in the decedent's taxable estate. The IRS looks at the "incidents of ownership" to determine who actually owned the policy.

"Incidents of ownership" include the right to change or name beneficiaries; borrow against the policy; pledge the cash reserve, if any; surrender, convert, or cancel the policy; and select the payment option for paying premiums. All of these reflect ownership rights. If the transferor retains these powers, the IRS will disallow the transfer and include the proceeds in the taxable estate.

In order to take out an insurance policy on another person, the purchaser must have an "insurable interest" in the insured. It is often difficult for gay or lesbian clients to establish an insurable interest in their partner. One way to do so is to show that the parties hold property together or are in business together. Joint property owners and business partners would have an insurable interest in the life of the other.

If an insurable interest cannot be established, a party can take out a policy and then, once it is issued, assign it to her partner. The partner then becomes responsible for paying all premiums. The partner also becomes the sole authority over the policy. The insured cannot force the partner to cancel the policy even if the parties split up.

The clients must inform the insurance company of the action taken. The transfer can take place, and be recognized, only if it is done with the knowledge of the insurer. The insurance company has the necessary forms required to make the transfer. Without following these formalities the insurer will have no record of the transfer and will not be obligated to honor it. As a result, the effort to transfer will be futile and the insurance proceeds will be included in the insured's taxable estate.

The insured can name anyone as the beneficiary and that designation cannot be challenged. It is another way that a gay or lesbian client can provide for a partner without going through probate and without worrying about a challenge.

A transfer of a life insurance policy constitutes a gift to the transferee. Policies with a present value of over $11,000 will have a gift tax assessed. A gift tax return will be required for the amount over $11,000. While the actual tax need not be paid immediately, the amount of the gift will be assessed against the lifetime exemption of $1 million.

Generally, one positive outcome is that the gift tax will be significantly less than the estate tax should the policy proceeds be left in the taxable estate.

It is important for the client to understand the present value or worth of the policy when contemplating a transfer. IRS rules provide that the gift value of a life insurance policy is its cost and not the cash surrender value.

Most insurance companies are able to provide an estimate of the gift tax value of a policy. This should be done before making the actual gift. Once made, the gift cannot be rescinded. Insurance companies can provide the form required by the IRS to be included with the gift tax return.

Transferring ownership of life insurance policies is a tactic that lesbian and gay clients need to know about. These clients want to take advantage of all available options to protect their assets and provide for each other.

In addition to transferring the policy to another person, the owner can also create an irrevocable life insurance trust. Once transferred, the trust owns the policy and has complete control over its administration.

There are requirements for a valid life insurance trust. The trust must be irrevocable. Any retention of rights will invalidate the trust for tax purposes. The owner of the policy cannot be the trustee. The trust must be established at least three years before the grantor's death, otherwise the trust will be discarded and the proceeds included in the taxable estate.

Transfer-on-Death Vehicle Certificates

Transfer-on-death vehicle certificates can be used to remove assets from the probate estate. These are statutory creatures and the statute is controlling. The statute will define what is meant by "vehicle." The definition can include automobiles, motorcycles, and boats.

The process for noting the transfer-on-death designation on the title is set forth in the statute. Most states authorize the Bureau of Motor Vehicles to handle the paperwork. By doing so the owner designates a person to receive title to the motor vehicle upon the owner's death. An official death certificate is needed to transfer title to the vehicle. The transfer is made outside of probate. The value of the vehicle is included in the decedent's overall estate for tax purposes, but probate is avoided.

A few states offer a vehicle TOD registration. Ohio, Missouri, and California have such a registration procedure.

Transfer-on-Death Deeds

The transfer-on-death deed permits a homeowner to provide for someone to receive title to the real estate after the owner's death. The property is transferred to the beneficiary outside of probate. This is similar to a survivorship deed; however, the homeowner does not relinquish any present ownership rights. The property is included in the estate for tax purposes.

Establishing a transfer-on-death deed or vehicle registration does not create a current interest in the property for the named beneficiary. Therefore, there is no gift tax because the gift is not complete. The owner of the property can change the beneficiary at any time without recourse by the beneficiary. This allows the owner to plan her estate while, at the same time, retaining control over her assets.

Chapter 6

Children

It has come to be known as the "gayby" boom. The American Bar Association's Family Law Section estimates that four million lesbian or gay parents are raising eight million to ten million children. The Lambda Legal Defense Fund estimates there are six million to ten million lesbian and gay parents raising six million to fourteen million children. And the National Adoption Information Clearinghouse estimates there are one and a half million to five million lesbian mothers and one million to three million gay fathers. Finally, the May 2000 edition of *Demography,* published by the Population Association of America, states that 21.6 percent of lesbian homes and 5.2 percent of gay male homes include children. All told, it adds up to lots of kids, lots of parents, and some unique, challenging, and often frustrating legal issues.

The issues facing lesbian and gay couples arise because the children involved are the product of adoption, artificial insemination, surrogate birth, or biological parenthood. In these cases only one party is recognized as the legal parent. The other partner is a legal stranger to the child. The question your clients will raise is how to become a family where both parties are legally recognized as the child's parents.

You will be seeing clients who want to know how they can protect their children since they cannot legally marry. It will be necessary to research your state law and court decisions to determine the current status. The Family Net section of the Human Rights Coalition, http://www.hrc.org/familynet, is a good source for information on family issues.

Without a legally protected parental relationship the child has

- No right to inherit from the nonbiological parent
- No right to receive Social Security benefits on that parent's account
- No right to receive health insurance benefits
- No right to other insurance benefits from that person's employer
- No right to have the nonbiological parent consent to needed emergency medical treatment or visit the child in the hospital

The legal landscape in this area is changing, mostly through judicial decisions. Lawyers are making creative arguments all the while concentrating on what is best for the child involved.

Courts are deciding these cases on the basis of the child's best interest. Since this is the general rule in custody and adoption cases, it is no surprise that the courts are finding ways to benefit the children of same-sex parents. Co-parent and second-parent adoptions give the child the legal security of having two parents.

Some courts are granting petitions for second-parent adoptions quietly. Others are calling in groups who oppose any extension of rights to lesbian and gay (LG) families. What amounts to a private action is, in some cases, evolving into a battle for children's rights.

The Ohio Supreme Court in *In re Bonfield*[1] granted a juvenile court jurisdiction to consider a joint custody arrangement for a lesbian couple. The court ruled in this manner even though Ohio law does not recognize a same-sex partner as a parent. The court also took the unusual step of revising the published decision after it was released. In the original decision the court stated that Ohio law prohibited second-parent adoptions. The revised decision removes this language. This is a significant step on the part of the court because it leaves the issue of second-parent adoptions open for now.

The basic protection to a child's well being is often defined as

- The right to inherit; intestacy rights
- The right to be guardian, conservator, or executor of the parent's estate
- The right to have the parent make medical decisions
- The right to be covered under the parent's health insurance plan
- The right to have the family unit protected under the Family and Medical Leave Act
- The right to sue for wrongful death
- The right to receive Social Security benefits as a dependent child
- The right to maintain a relationship with the parent
- The right to receive financial support during the child's minority

When the biological parent dies, the state may place the child in a foster home or with relatives with whom she is unfamiliar, rather than with the other parent. This can be avoided by taking steps discussed in this chapter. Every child is entitled to the emotional security inherent in the legal recognition of family relationships.

---

1. 96 Ohio St. 3d 218 (2002).

Questions to Ask

One of the first questions to ask a client is, "Who are the parents?" The answer could surprise you. In this day of in vitro fertilization and surrogacy, there may be four parents involved and not just the two people sitting before you. Sometimes a gay man will enter a legal marriage with a lesbian in order to start a family. The parties then continue their relationships with their same-sex partners all the while raising the children of the "marriage."

Another scenario may involve a gay male couple hiring a surrogate mother to have their child. The surrogate mother may be a lesbian who intends to remain a part of the child's life. Alter the sex and you can have a lesbian couple entering into an agreement with a gay male to father their children. The man may be the father of children birthed by both women.

Yet another possibility is that a male friend agrees to be the father. Initially, he agrees to forfeit all parental rights to the child, until his son is born. He always wanted a son, so now he wants to be involved.

It is important to know the players. It is essential to understand the nuances that exist in this family unit. Your clients may not meet any definition of "family" you ever considered. But we are talking about families and your clients will want to know how to protect them.

There are parenting agreements the parties can execute to spell out their intentions. Your clients may want to seek a second-parent adoption. You need to research your state law to determine if it is feasible.

Another alternative is to consider the local judges. In some cases, judges have granted these adoptions, quietly and without fanfare.

Shared-Parenting Agreements

The purpose of shared-parenting agreements is to establish a written record of the parties' intentions concerning their children. While these agreements are private in nature and, usually, not sanctioned by a court, they do provide a record the parties can refer to should a dispute arise.

Any shared-parenting agreement must clearly state the couple's intention to continue to co-parent even if their relationship ends. The agreement should include provisions dealing with custody, visitation, child support, college tuition, and the like.

The agreement can also be used to establish the nature of the relationship between the nonlegal parent and the child. There are numerous cases in which a same-sex couple petitions a court to determine custody, visitation, and support. As with heterosexual couples, relationships end and the children become a factor in the post-relationship world.

A shared-parenting agreement may be used to assist the court in reaching a decision. There is no guarantee these agreements will be recognized by the court. Unfortunately, there are many cases in which the legal parent uses the existing laws to deny the former partner any contact with a child. This occurs even in cases where the former partner and child developed a strong bond.

These are difficult cases because there are few, if any, guidelines to follow. This is virgin territory and attorneys must call upon all their resources to meet their client's needs and achieve their goals.

A sample shared-parenting agreement is included in Appendix A.

Second-Parent Adoption

Second-parent adoption is the preferred method of adoption for same-sex couples. Second-parent adoptions permit the second parent to adopt without the first parent relinquishing any legal or parental rights. This results in the child having two legal parents. It also grants the adoptive parents the same custody, support, and visitation rights as those enjoyed by biological parents or stepparents.

Second-parent adoptions usually occur when one partner is the biological parent or has already adopted a child. Second-parent adoptions are not possible when the child is from a previous heterosexual relationship and the other biological parent retains parental rights. This type of adoption also does not work when the sperm donor has not waived his parental rights. In that case the donor is the child's legal father. This would also be true in a surrogacy case where the biological mother has not relinquished her parental rights.

There are advantages for the child in second-parent adoptions:

- The custody rights of the second parent are guaranteed if the other parent dies or becomes incapacitated
- The child enjoys additional financial security because he will be eligible for Social Security survivor benefits if the second parent dies
- The child is also a recognized heir of the second parent
- The child is eligible for health benefits from the second parent
- The child is entitled to financial support from the second parent if the couple separates

Appellate courts in some states have approved second-parent adoptions. These states are California, Illinois, Indiana, Massachusetts, Pennsylvania, New Jersey, New York, and Vermont, and the District of Columbia. In addition, California, Vermont, and Connecticut have statutes that explicitly permit second-parent adoptions.

The Pennsylvania Supreme Court ruled in August 2002 that second-parent adoptions are permitted under the state's adoption law. The court held in a unanimous decision that "[t]here is no language in the Adoption Act precluding two unmarried same-sex partners . . . from adopting a child who had no legal parents. It is, therefore, absurd to prohibit their adoption merely because their children were the biological or adopted children of one of the partners prior to the filing of the adoption petition."[2]

The appellate courts in Colorado, Nebraska, and Wisconsin issued decisions refusing to permit second-parent adoptions because they are not provided for in state law. The Nebraska Court of Appeals, however, ruled in 2002 that a second-parent adoption granted in Pennsylvania must be recognized in Nebraska.[3] This appears to be the only appellate court to address the issue.

Trial judges throughout the country are exercising judicial discretion and granting second-parent adoptions. The decisions were issued in Alabama, Alaska, Delaware, Hawaii, Illinois, Indiana, Iowa, Louisiana, Maryland, Minnesota, Nevada, New Mexico, Oregon, Rhode Island, Texas, and Washington.

Florida is one state that expressly prohibits lesbians and gays from adopting children. The statute is being challenged in federal court at this time. The case, *Lofton v. Kearney*,[4] involves gay foster parents who want to adopt their foster children. Ironically, Florida law does not prohibit gay men and lesbians from becoming foster parents. The U.S. District Court dismissed the case and it is now on appeal to the Eleventh Circuit Court of Appeals.

An issue arises about the validity of a second-parent adoption granted by a county probate judge without explicit statutory authority. A general rule of law is that a validly entered adoption decree is, unless set aside by an appellate court, valid. A guardian who believes it is not in the child's best interests or a biological parent whose rights were terminated may bring the appeal.

---

2. *In re* Adoption of R.B.F. and R.C.F. and *In re* Adoption of C.C.G. and Z.C.G., No J-100-2002, 2002, WL 1906000 (Pa. Aug. 20, 2002).
3. Russell v. Bridgens, 264 Neb. 217; 647 N.W.2d 56 (2002).
4. 157 F. Supp. 2d 1372 (S.D. Fla. 2001).

Without an appeal, however, the order can be considered secure. All states have mandatory appeal periods, and failure to bring an appeal within those periods will forever preclude a challenge.

In Ohio, a challenge to an adoption decree must be made within twelve months. After that time, no adoption of a minor child can be questioned or legally challenged for any reason. This includes an allegation of fraud.

Standby Guardian

The legal parent can do a great service to her child by providing for, in writing, a standby guardian. If the parent should die the child may be placed in foster care until the state court has the opportunity to decide that child's fate. The trauma faced by a child in this situation is unimaginable. Since the parent's partner is a legal stranger to the child there is no automatic right to custody of the child.

Specifying a standby guardian will provide the authorities with an alternative to placing the child in foster care. If the child is not placed in foster care, she may be placed with relatives of the deceased parent. These may be people with whom the child has no relationship. The goal is to protect the child and provide for the child's best interests. A standby guardian designation will help ensure continuity in the child's life at a most difficult time.

Illinois and New York permit the appointment of a standby guardian and will grant immediate custody of the child to that person. This is a temporary order that continues until the court can address the child's future. It can also serve as a bridge until the will is probated. If the deceased parent's partner is named as the child's guardian in a will, the standby guardian stipulation follows the decedent's expressed interest.

Testamentary Provisions

Couples with children need an estate plan to provide for those children. While same-sex couples are no different from other parents, there is one exception. In most cases involving same-sex couples, only one member of the couple is considered to be the "legal parent."

Both parties can provide for a child in a will. While the nonlegal parent cannot nominate a guardian in her will, she can provide for the child as a beneficiary under the will. The best way to accomplish this would be to establish a trust for the child. This allows the testator to control the disposition of the assets to the child. It also prevents someone the testator does not approve of from having access to the child's estate.

Naming a guardian is one of the most important components of a will when minor children are concerned. It gives the parent the opportunity to name the person or persons who will be responsible for the child after the parent's death. The nomination is considered guidance to a court. There is no guarantee that court will select the person nominated in the will.

The guardian provision can stipulate who will be the guardian of the person and of the estate. This can be the same person but it is advisable to specify the nomination separately. This can help the proposed guardian retain the authority over the child's estate in cases where the court refuses to name the nominee as guardian of the person.

Some courts, exhibiting animus toward the parties' relationship, refuse to name a same-sex partner as a child's guardian. The court has less reason to oppose naming the partner as the guardian of the estate.

By specifically naming the nonbiological parent as the guardian of the estate, the legal parent ensures continued contact between the partner and the child. It may be advisable to expressly state that the guardian has the authority and responsibility to contact the child on a regular basis. As guardian of the minor child's estate, she handles all decisions concerning the dispersal of funds for the child.

Difficult Issues

Obtaining legal protection for a parental relationship is not just for the benefit of the adults involved. The primary beneficiary of these arrangements is the child. Without a legally recognized parental relationship, where both members of a same-sex couple are designated legal parents, the child suffers in a variety of ways.

The child has no legal right to inherit from the parent designated a "legal stranger." The child cannot obtain Social Security survivor benefits should the nonlegal parent die. Equally important is that the child cannot be placed on the health insurance plan of the nonlegal parent. If the legal parent does not have health insurance, the child is one of the millions of uninsured children in the country.

With no legal standing the nonlegal parent cannot give her consent for emergency treatment should it be required. Visitation in the emergency room may be prohibited because the partner does not qualify as a "parent." All of this harms the child. These are only a few of the benefits denied a child because one caregiver is considered a legal stranger.

"Psychological Parent"

A new classification is being formed to define the nonlegal parent: "psychological parent." This can be the nonbiological parent who is living with the child. It is a new argument being made in an attempt to benefit the child. There are some lawyers who are petitioning on behalf of the psychological parent for guardianship. This does not terminate the biological parent's rights but can serve the purpose of gaining medical coverage for the child.

In some states, including Missouri, the natural parent must be found to be "unfit, unwilling, or unable" to perform the functions of a parent before a guardianship will be granted.

The child cannot inherit from a psychological parent who dies intestate. Further, the psychological parent cannot designate a guardian in her will.

In Colorado, the parents (psychological and biological) are allowed to file an uncontested petition that seeks an allocation of parental responsibilities. This petition can include a parenting plan.

Ironically, most cases seeking adoption or shared-parenting plans are uncontested. The challenge comes from outsiders or judges who refuse to put aside their own prejudices in order to determine the child's best interests. But some courts are beginning to consider the child's best interest in relation to the psychological parent.

Courts are beginning to consider the child's rights to parenting time, independent of what the biological parent may want. Example: A family court in New York[5] permitted a foster mother to visit with the child she cared for from birth over the biological father's objections. The court allowed the visitation because the child had a First Amendment right and due process interest in visitation regardless of the parent's opposition. The court decided that the child had a fundamental right to maintain contact with the person with whom he had developed a parentlike relationship. In this case, the foster mother had risen to the level of a psychological parent. The court found it was in the child's best interest to continue contact even when the parent objected.

Liberty interests are protected by the due process clauses of both the federal and state constitutions. However, there is a presumption that the decision

---

5. Webster v. Ryan, 729 N.Y.S.2d 315 (Fam. Ct. 2001).

to terminate or restrict the contact is in the child's best interest. This is where a child can benefit from having an attorney appointed to represent him in a court proceeding.

Life-Planning Issues

In addition to the agreements and provisions mentioned above, there are other documents a same-sex couple will want to execute to protect a child.

The biological parent will want to execute an authorization for medical care of a minor naming her partner as the person allowed to consent to medical treatment. A durable power of attorney may also include such a provision, but it is generally better to have a separate, clearly written document. The psychological parent needs to keep an original on hand at all times.

Traveling may pose problems for a same-sex couple with children. Example: A lesbian couple found themselves being interrogated by personnel from a U.S. airline when they attempted to travel to Mexico on vacation. Airline personnel demanded to see documentation from the children's father allowing the women to remove the children from the United States. This was a public confrontation in full view and hearing of the children.

The airline's employees could not understand how two women could have two children if there was no father involved. The women explained that the children were conceived through in vitro fertilization. The airline personnel told them there was a possibility they would not be allowed into Mexico or back into the United States on their return. These women, and their children, were U.S. citizens.

How does one deal with such ignorance? Your clients may want to consider worst-case scenarios when traveling, particularly in the present climate of suspicion and overreaction. A notarized statement that the children were conceived by artificial insemination may seem unnecessary, unless your clients run into ill-trained airline employees. Gay male couples may be subject to even greater scrutiny because of a general suspicion about men traveling with children. This may be particularly true if there is no familial resemblance.

Lesbian and gay couples must also deal with school authorities. This is best handled on the first day of registration. Explaining the nature of the family to school officials will alleviate future problems. A formal, written statement, signed by the biological parent, authorizing the school to consider the psychological parent to have the same standing as the parent would be helpful. The authorization should specify that the parent's partner is an emergency contact on an equal footing with the parent. Taking the time to draft these statements will help the couple to plan for all contingencies. Include parent-teacher conferences, signing report cards, and attendance at school functions in the authorization. Use a catchall phrase such as "And any other situations, incidents, functions, or similar possibilities where a parent is needed by school officials." Review it with the school principal to determine if something should be added or clarified. This will help the child, the school, and the parents.

You might even consider putting your contact information on the statement in the event questions are raised, or, in the alternative, note that you prepared the document. Sometimes having a lawyer's name on a document can forestall problems.

Chapter 7

Essential Estate Planning Documents

Unlike married couples, same-sex couples must take additional steps to ensure their wishes are followed. Most of the documents discussed in this chapter relate to health care. It is in health care situations that many same-sex couples have the most difficulty. Many birth families try to exclude the partner from having contact with or influencing the patient's care. Few states have laws that protect same-sex couples in health care situations. These documents may provide what the law refuses to provide.

Health Care Powers of Attorney and Living Wills

Health care powers of attorney (HCPOAs) and living wills (also known as advance directives) are essential for same-sex couples. Without them medical providers and medical institutions will look to blood relatives for health care guidance. The patient's partner will not be consulted and may be—and, in fact, often is—prevented from visiting.

Many states developed their own forms to be used by individuals. Same-sex couples face a potential problem while traveling. Your clients should carry original documents with them. There will be no assumption that either of them is authorized to make health care decisions for the other.

Many hospitals have policies that limit visitation to "immediate family only." And they do not include same-sex partners in that category. This, however, is contrary to the national hospital accreditation standards published by the Joint Commission on Accreditation of Healthcare Organizations (JCAHO). JCAHO defines "family" as "The person(s) who plays a significant role in the individual's [patient's] life. This may include a person(s) not legally related to the individual."[1]

---

1. Joint Commission Resources JCR, *2001 Hospital Accreditation Standards*, p. 322.

"Do Not Resuscitate" (DNR) instructions may be included in living wills and health care powers of attorney. Some state forms include this authority as a standard provision. The attorney-in-fact for health care decisions is authorized to instruct medical personnel to add a DNR notation to the patient's chart.

A good rule of thumb is to have the clients execute multiple original documents of the HCPOA and living will. This reduces the possibility of someone challenging the legitimacy of a copy. It is also advisable to have the client sign the document in blue rather than black ink. This prevents someone from questioning whether the document is an original or a copy.

Attorneys should use the forms prepared by the state. Hospitals and health care providers recognize the "official" documents. They may include seals from the state bar association and state medical association. Using the preprinted documents, rather than preparing one on your letterhead, may give a level of comfort to the health care provider—the familiarity with a form. This is not to say that you cannot add specific instructions requested by the client.

Whenever possible, the clients should discuss their plans with their families and document those discussions. This also serves to preempt future challenges. If the client is estranged from his family, a letter sent by certified mail, return receipt requested, might be useful to defend against a future challenge based on "My brother would never do that." In fact, a written confirmation of the discussion also helps memorialize the conversation and can serve to refute future denials by the family.

Recently, new regulations and procedures went into effect under the Health Insurance Portability and Accountability Act of 1996 (HIPAA). The federal rules are the first to limit the release of health care information by health care providers. The point of the HIPAA rules is to protect patient privacy, not from their families and designated agents, but from entities with no reason to need the information. However, the rules are so new that many doctors and hospitals are taking a conservative, limited approach to the dissemination of medical information and denying information to everyone.

The rules place a high premium on patient privacy. Violations of these rules constitute a federal offense. The HIPAA rules may interfere with a lesbian or gay couple's health care and living will designations. This includes any other documents the couple drafts that may require access to health care decisions.

Therefore, it may be necessary to include language in the various documents to address any HIPAA concerns. The language should expressly authorize the health care provider to release all medical information to the designated person. Explicit language will go far in ensuring the designated agent's access to information.

Including such language in a preexisting form may be insufficient to meet HIPAA requirements. Therefore, Appendix A includes a form clients can use to authorize the release of health information under HIPAA.

Designation of Agent

One way to give your clients some peace of mind is with a visitation authorization. Preparing a document that designates who is authorized to visit may save your clients grief and aggravation when faced with ignorant personnel. The document can authorize visitation in hospitals, nursing homes, hospices, and other health care institutions. Your client's signature on these documents creates a paper trail that establishes the client's intent in this regard. Granted, all the documents in the world will not help anyone if the institution is bound and determined to ignore them. However, it may make the institution's personnel think twice about their actions.

You may want to include a reference to the JCAHO regulations in the body of the document. That way, you are referencing an organization with which medical personnel are familiar. Do not forget to include a reference to the fact that a lawyer created the documents. That might be additional incentive to honor the patient's wishes.

The visitation authorization can also stipulate who is not welcome to visit. This may alleviate nasty hallway arguments. It also further establishes the patient-partner's desires, wishes, and intent.

Both partners should also execute documents that provide for the custody and disposition of their remains and personal property. This document can also include a designation of who is permitted to authorize an autopsy. This comes into play when an autopsy is optional or discretionary.

It is possible to make these separate documents; however, combining them limits the number of documents the client must account for or remember to bring. See Appendix A for a sample form.

Funeral Arrangements

Funeral arrangements are another area requiring serious thought if the couple wants to ensure their wishes are honored. In many states the law authorizes the decedent's next of kin to make funeral arrangements. This includes over-riding the decedent's own arrangements, such as a prepaid funeral contract, made prior to death. This can be a problem if the family wins the race to the funeral home and signs the contract. The estate is presumed to be responsible for the cost of the funeral.

One suggestion to deter interference with the decedent's funeral arrange-ments is to include a clause in the will restricting payment to only those expenses that are specified by the decedent. The testator can include an instruction that orders her executor to refuse to pay any bills associated with a funeral that deviates from her expressed wishes.

Will it work? A legitimate argument can be made that the next of kin has the right to make alternative funeral arrangements but has no right to expect the estate to pay the bill. Another facet of the argument is under contract law. The contract is between the funeral home and the person signing the contract, but the funeral home can file a claim against the estate. Putting the funeral provider on notice of the decedent's expressed wishes and the executor's intent to oppose any claim may cause the provider to rethink its position.

One problem with putting the instructions in the will is that the funeral is usually over before the will is opened. A better method is to include the instructions in a separate document as well as in the will—particularly in regard to limiting the executor's authority to pay for anything that does not conform to the decedent's instructions.

Further, the executor has a fiduciary duty to the heirs to manage the estate in a reasonable manner. Paying for a funeral that does not comport with the decedent's wishes may constitute a breach of the executor's fiduciary duty to preserve the estate.

Without written funeral instructions, nearly every state gives control of those arrangements to blood relatives. The surviving partner will be powerless and may even be barred from the services. A prepaid funeral may alleviate the problem. This needs to be considered since a funeral home may not listen to someone named as the executor but not yet appointed.

It is important, therefore, to understand state law concerning funerals. Questions to ask include

- Who has the right to control the funeral?
- What is the burden of proof?
- Are there limits on liability?
- Who has standing to sue?

This last question is of importance in lesbian and gay (LG) relationships because it comes into play if the family refuses to honor the decedent's funeral wishes. There are some standard claims that can be raised in these cases. They include claims for mental anguish and mishandling of remains. Cremation disputes are also claims that arise.

It is important to remember that the Federal Trade Commission's Funeral Rule[2] governs only providers who sell both goods and services. Therefore, prepaid funeral arrangements are not covered by that rule. The FTC is considering an amendment to this rule to deal with this loophole.

Mental anguish is a possible claim, but the surviving partner will have to show gross negligence or an intentional or outrageous act. It is rare to recover damages in these cases.

A funeral director may be liable for breach of a personal services contract. This cause of action does not require either an outrageous or intentional act.

Another area of controversy is in the cemetery itself. Cemetery abuses are widespread and common. This happens because this is one of the least regulated industries in the country. Since there is no contract between the cemetery and the family, the executor may be the only one with standing to sue.

Guardian/Conservator Nomination

Nominating a guardian or conservator is another step your clients can take. A nomination of guardian/conservator may be an addendum to the health care power of attorney. There have been occasions where parents or other family members contest the right of a nontraditional partner to care for her partner. The family usually argues that the incompetent partner never indicated her preference. This document provides written proof of the principal's intent. See Appendix A for a sample form.

Durable Power of Attorney for Finances

Clients can provide for the continuation of their affairs in their absence or during a disability through a durable power of attorney (DPOA) for finances. These agreements can be used by individuals or couples to ensure that their bank accounts, property, and other assets are properly managed if they become unable to do so directly. This document can also preclude the need

---

2. 16 C.F.R. pt. 453.

for a guardianship. The power of attorney is effective only during the life of the grantor. It can be rescinded at any time, preferably in writing. Some states permit these documents to be recorded. If it is, any rescission should also be recorded and original copies recovered. The power in the document becomes effective immediately upon signing, unless there are restrictions contained in the DPOA's language.

Couples in a committed relationship often execute mutual DPOAs. In these situations, it is advisable to recommend, in the strongest terms possible, that the parties also execute a domestic partnership agreement.

Clients must be aware of the power inherent in these documents. Most people do not understand what a power of attorney means from a legal and practical standpoint.

Long-term same-sex couples act as one. This type of document allows them to continue in that vein should one become incapacitated. It also provides another piece of evidence of their relationship and their intentions.

The DPOA for finances can include language to create a springing power of attorney, one that will come into effect only upon a condition precedent being met. The principal's doctor will need to write a letter attesting to the fact that the principal is no longer capable of managing his affairs. This can be tricky, but language in the power of attorney can be included to overcome objections.

See Appendix A for samples of a DPOA for finances and springing power of attorney language.

Business Powers of Attorney

Many lesbians and gay men own a business. Drafting a business power of attorney for these clients provides them with a planning tool designed to help their business. Clients who have extensive business dealings or partnerships need to ensure that decisions are made when needed. Clients who have a revocable living trust may want to use the trustee as their business attorney-in-fact. Generally speaking, it is inadvisable to have the person named in the health care power of attorney serve as the attorney-in-fact under the business power of attorney.

Your client may also want to prepare a buy-sell agreement for the business. This will set forth the specifics of business divestiture. Such an agreement can be used to address questions about the future of the business.

Government Accounts

Federal employees under the Federal Employee Retirement System (FERS) are entitled to participate in the Thrift Savings Plan (TSP). In 2004, employees are able to contribute 14 percent of their pre-tax income to the plan. The government provides a maximum match to 5 percent. A federal employee can designate her same-sex partner as the beneficiary of the TSP account.

There is no provision in federal law that allows an employee to name a domestic partner as a beneficiary of a retirement plan (FERS or Civil Service Retirement System, CSRS). Once the employee dies, the pension payments stop. The same is true for all other federal employee retirement plans, military or civilian.

Further, a surviving domestic partner cannot claim Social Security survivor benefits on the decedent's account. And, the nonlegal children of the decedent are ineligible for surviving child benefits.

The issues facing LG clients in planning their estates are many. It is the attorney's job to cover all the bases in an attempt to draft documents that reflect the client's intent. Lesbian and gay individuals and couples face additional problems if the family refuses to accept their relative's sexual orientation and the relationship. The last thing the surviving partner needs is to deal with a hostile family.

Same-sex couples require a variety of documents that provide evidence of their relationship and their intentions. Some people refuse to believe that their relative is/was gay or that they would want this "person" caring for them. It is for the parties' peace of mind that we draft these documents. This is why it is so important to talk to your clients at length to get a feel for their family situation. You cannot adequately advise your clients if you do not understand their fears about the future.

Chapter 8

Lesbian and Gay Seniors

Ageism isolates seniors in mainstream society. It is an even greater problem in lesbian and gay communities because seniors are even more invisible. Seniors in the lesbian and gay community came of age in a different time. Most kept their personal lives under wraps and, even now with people being "openly gay," they are still reluctant to go public. Example: A gay male couple recently celebrated fifty-five years together, yet they still refer to each other as "my friend."

Even when lesbian and gay (LG) seniors feel safe enough to be "out" they often find it necessary to return to the closet when in need of services from the heterosexual senior community and its service providers.

A 1994 New York State survey found that gay elders were unwelcome at 46 percent of senior centers. That percentage increased to 50 percent in a 1999 New York survey. Many services to seniors are concentrated in senior centers. If LG seniors are not welcome in those venues, their ability to obtain services is adversely affected.

There are a limited number of retirement communities that welcome LG seniors. Many retirement communities will not accept a lesbian or gay individual or couple.

A few retirement communities cater to LG seniors. The existing ones are located in Florida, Arizona, and New Mexico. Plans are in place for retirement developments in Cleveland, Los Angeles, San Francisco, and North Carolina. Some LG seniors do not want to restrict themselves to a same-sex development, but, with a growing senior population, these arrangements will continue to grow in popularity.

The 2000 census identified more than fifty-six million U.S. residents who are older than age fifty-five. The Bureau of the Census predicts those numbers will increase substantially through 2020. The boomers are entering their golden years, and many are lesbian or gay. It is estimated that three million Americans over the age of sixty are lesbian or gay. That is 8 percent of the population. By 2030, one in five Americans will be sixty-five or older and approximately five million will be lesbian or gay.

Many of those elderly LG persons will be veterans. "Don't ask, don't tell" aside, thousands of lesbians and gay men have served honorably in our nation's armed forces. They are entitled to military retired pay, health care, and other veterans' benefits. Yet they may be subjected to anti-gay attitudes by staff and patients at Veterans Health Administration hospitals.

Medicaid is the largest single payor of direct medical services for persons with AIDS (PWAs) and children with AIDS. The Department of Health and Human Services estimates that 50 percent of PWAs and 90 percent of children with AIDS receive medical services through Medicaid.

No one is taking the lead in talking about or resolving the growing problem of an aging population and its cumulative effect on the nation's resources. This problem does not solely affect LG seniors; however, these seniors will be affected because there is still limited legal protection on the basis of sexual orientation.

The types of legal issues affecting older Americans are growing. These include

- Medicare and Medicaid
- Public benefits
- Social Security
- Advance directives
- Financial and physical abuse
- Discrimination by age, gender, and sexual orientation
- long-term care availability
- Rise in nursing home litigation

Lawyers representing LG senior clients must be aware of the problems they face. For example, there are no Social Security survivor benefits for the surviving partner of a lesbian or gay client. Social Security provides survivor benefits only for a spouse or dependent child.

If one partner needs to enter a nursing home, Medicaid rules consider that person to be single for purposes of determining eligibility. There is no "community spouse" provision for the partner of a lesbian or gay nursing home resident. In order to qualify for Medicaid, the partner entering the nursing home must spend down to the required level, usually $1,500. This can have a devastating effect on the other partner. Yet that person's predicament is not considered.

The unequal treatment does not stop or start with federal benefits. The named beneficiary of a 401(k) plan cannot roll over the proceeds into an Individual Retirement Account without being subjected to a 20 percent tax bite, a penalty that a legal spouse would not have to pay.

Federal law requires pension plans to protect spouses. There is no similar requirement to protect same-sex partners, because "domestic partners" are not synonymous with "spouses."

This discrimination came home to the partner of a Tampa police officer after her partner was killed in the line of duty.

On July 6, 2001, Master Patrol Officer Lois Marrero was shot and killed on duty with the Tampa Police Department. She died fifteen months from retirement. Ms. Marrero left behind her partner of eleven years, Tampa Police Officer Mickie Mashburn.

Unlike the officer's heterosexual counterparts, Ms. Mashburn was not entitled to receive any part of Ms. Marrero's pension. Florida's pension law provides that only spouses and children are eligible to receive survivor benefits. She also could not receive a refund of the $50,000 paid into the pension fund by Ms. Marrero. The eight-member city pension board rejected Ms. Mashburn's application and awarded the $50,000 refund of pension premiums to Ms. Marrero's mother. Ms. Marrero's family claimed there was no relationship between Ms. Marrero and Ms. Mashburn. And, since Ms. Marrero died intestate, her parents inherited her estate.

Ms. Mashburn did receive $25,000 from the Florida crime victims' compensation fund. Florida Attorney General Bob Butterworth approved that payment.

The National Center for Lesbian Rights is representing Ms. Mashburn in a lawsuit challenging the pension board's decision. The Tampa City Council is reviewing the pension policy. Ms. Mashburn has the support of the police and firefighter unions.

There is no federal legislation banning discrimination based on sexual orientation in employment, housing, or public accommodations. Absent state law restrictions, nursing homes and assisted living facilities are free to discriminate against LG elders in their admission policies.

Even when services and benefits are available, many LG seniors are unaware either of their existence or of the eligibility requirements. This is where good lawyers come into play. In 2001 the federal Office on Aging recognized that lesbian and gay elders in the United States are underserved by the Older Americans Act. The recognition is a start; however, to date Congress is not considering any legislation that will remedy the situation.

Lawyers can determine a client's eligibility for federal and state benefits at the Web site http://www.benefitscheckup.org. The National Council on Aging, a nonprofit group in Washington, D.C., set up this site in June 2001.

For some lesbians and gay men, an assisted living facility may be a feasible alternative to nursing home care. However, neither state nor federal governments regulate assisted living facilities. These are private-pay facilities; residents do not qualify for Medicaid. The facilities generally provide limited resources and may lack qualified medical personnel to dispense medications. These facilities are often not licensed or equipped to deal with a resident's medical needs. And, on top of everything else, these are for-profit operations.

Older Americans Act

The Older Americans Act (OAA),[1] enacted in 1965 and reauthorized in 2000, provides services for Americans over age sixty. The reauthorization extends the act's programs through fiscal year 2005.

According to the U.S. Administration on Aging, forty-four million Americans are age sixty or older. The OAA is the primary vehicle for the organization, coordination, and provision of community-based services for older Americans and their families.

The OAA provides a variety of services, including home-delivered meals, health screenings and counseling, abuse protection, volunteer guardians, and legal services. In addition, eligible seniors may be able to get help with minor home repairs, yard work, housekeeping, and respite care.

The reauthorized OAA includes a new program, the National Family Caregiver Support Program (NFCSP). This is designed to help family caregivers of older adults who are ill or who have disabilities. Two-thirds of non-institutionalized persons rely on family and friends for assistance with daily living activities. One-quarter supplement family care with services from paid providers.

The NFCSP provides grants to state agencies on aging to work with Area Agencies on Aging and service and community organizations to provide support services. These services include

---

1. Pub. L. No. 106-501 (Nov. 13, 2000).

- Information to caregivers about available services
- Assistance in gaining access to services
- Counseling, support groups, and caregiver training
- Respite care
- Supplemental services to complement that care being given

The OAA also maintains the original objectives that serve to preserve the rights and dignity of older Americans. There are provisions for low-income members of minority groups and an added focus on older individuals living in rural areas.

This act can be a source of assistance for LG elders who remain in the community. Clients who need assistance, or their caregivers, should contact their local Area Agency on Aging for more information. They can also contact the U.S. Administration on Aging through its Web site, http://www.aoa.gov.

The Eldercare Locator (http://www.eldercare.gov, 800-677-1116), a public service of the Adminstration on Aging, is designed to help find appropriate community resources for seniors.

Nursing Home Care

Statistics from the Administration on Aging show that at least 40 percent of people turning sixty-five will stay in a nursing home at least once in their lifetime. Half will stay six months or less. One in five will stay a year or more and one in ten will stay three years or longer. Most of those over age sixty-five are women. Given these figures, it is likely you will have clients who will need nursing home care at some point in their lives.

According to *Consumer Reports,* 36 percent of assisted living residents enter a nursing home because their needs cannot be accommodated. Two percent enter a nursing home because they run out of money.

A percentage of those older persons entering nursing homes will be lesbians and gay men.

Since there is no legal sanction against sexual-orientation discrimination, it is important to determine if the nursing home accepts lesbian and gay residents. Does the facility treat a same-sex couple the same as a married couple? Is a same-sex couple allowed to reside in a couple's room? These are important questions to ask *before* the person enters a nursing home or assisted living facility. Too often an openly lesbian or gay couple or individual will be forced back into the closet in order to be accepted into a nursing home community.

Nursing home or retirement facilities can deny entry to the elderly lesbian or gay person because of sexual orientation. Housing is one of the most important concerns facing LG seniors. A situation arose in Florida when a lesbian couple was denied admission to the Westminster Oaks Retirement Community. The facility had a policy against unmarried, nonrelated couples living together.

Florida, however, is one state in which county and local governments have enacted legislation that prohibits housing discrimination based on sexual orientation. In the Westminster Oaks case, the policy violates a local law protecting lesbians and gay men from housing discrimination. The same law includes prohibitions against discrimination based on gender and marital status. The National Center for Lesbian Rights has filed discrimination charges against Westminster Oaks on behalf of the women involved.

Another Florida case, originating in Boca Raton, involved an apartment complex that refused to rent an apartment to a gay couple. This action violated a county law that protects same-sex couples from housing discrimination. The apartment complex, Colonial Apartments, settled the matter during mediation and agreed to pay $25,000 to each of the men and to Lambda Legal Defense and Education Fund.

Another consideration is to address a person's right to privacy in the facility. While many LG individuals and couples are open about their relationships, many others remain closeted. It is important to your client that a facility honors that person's right to privacy. Outing an elderly lesbian or gay man can be devastating. This is particularly true if the threatened outing is used for nefarious purposes such as blackmail or to prevent the senior resident from complaining about his or her treatment.

Even residents who are open about their sexuality may be subjected to discriminatory conduct by the nursing home staff. In one instance, the nursing home staff refused to bathe an elderly nursing home resident because they did not want to touch "the lesbian."

In many nursing home facilities sexuality is often a problem for the staff. No one wants to think of these "old folks" being sexually active. Many consider gay sex to be deviant behavior.

Each state's Agency on Aging must create an Office of Long-Term Care Ombudsman. This office provides help and information to elderly persons and their families and friends. The office is also charged with visiting nursing homes, receiving and investigating complaints, and providing information on long-term care facilities. The ombudsman office is also a good source of current information on local nursing homes.

The state Department of Health is responsible for issuing regulations governing nursing home operations. There is also a federal mandate requiring nursing homes to ensure that each resident is able to maintain, as much as possible, the quality of life at the level enjoyed before entering the facility.

Health Care Issues Affecting Lesbian and Gay Seniors

Throughout the country health care is a concern. This is not just an issue for lesbians and gay men. It affects everyone. But lesbians and gay men have additional medical concerns that do not affect the general population.

The first concern is doctor bias. Many lesbians do not seek medical assistance because they have experienced bias from homophobic doctors. As with a lawyer, it is essential for a patient to be open and honest with her doctor. If she cannot tell the doctor that she is a lesbian, the quality of care will suffer. For example, women of childbearing age are always asked about the type of birth control used. Lesbians use the only kind that is 100 percent effective; they do not have sex with men. While the "gayby" boom is in full swing there are still many more lesbians who, in response to the question "Are you pregnant?," will answer, "Not unless you've seen a star in the east!"

In addition to the possibility of reduced medical care, lesbians and gay men experience stress arising from homophobia, the fear of being outed, and the fear of being the victim of violence inspired by hate. This situation is even greater when the person is elderly and less able to withstand the assault on senses and person.

Elderly lesbians and gay men are very concerned about the availability of health insurance. Most of these elders are not entitled to supplemental coverage from their partners. Also, as stated earlier, Medicaid treats same-sex couples differently from married heterosexual couples under its regulations. An increasing number of corporations and companies of all sizes are offering health insurance and other benefits to same-sex couples. It is something for lawyers representing LG elder clients to investigate.

As a result of these concerns it is important for lawyers to ensure that their clients are provided with all the legal documents necessary to protect them in a health care facility. This includes hospitals, nursing homes, assisted living facilities, home health care situations, and the like. It is also important for lawyers to determine that their clients are being treated with respect and that their needs are being met.

Social Security

The Old Age, Survivors and Disability Insurance program (OASDI)[2] is specific concerning eligibility for survivor benefits. There are no Social Security benefits available to the surviving partner of a same-sex couple. This includes retirement benefits, disability benefits, and Supplemental Security Income (SSI). Clients must be made aware that a domestic partnership agreement does not confer any federal benefits on a surviving partner.

However, the Social Security statute includes a definition of "family status" that your clients may fall under in very specific circumstances. 42 U.S.C. § 416(h)(1)(A) of the statute reads as follows:

(h) Determination of family status

(1)(A)(i) An applicant is the wife, husband, widow, or widower of a fully or currently insured individual for purposes of this subchapter if the courts of the State in which such insured individual is domiciled at the time such applicant files an application, or, if such insured individual is dead, the courts of the State in which he was domiciled at the time of death, or, if such insured is or was not so domiciled in any State, the courts of the District of Columbia, would find that such applicant and such insured individual were validly married at the time such applicant files such application or, if such insured individual is dead, at the time he died.

(ii) *If such courts do not find that such applicant and such insured individual were validly married at such time, such applicant shall, nevertheless be deemed to be the wife, husband, widow, or widower, as the case may be, of such insured individual if such applicant would, under the laws applied by such courts in determining the devolution of intestate personal property, have the same status with respect to the taking of such property as a wife, husband, widow, or widower of such insured individual.* (emphasis added)

The key language is in Subsection (1)(A)(ii). If an applicant and the insured individual were entitled to the insured's intestate property under state law, and the state law considers the partner to be a "spouse," then the applicant may be eligible to apply for benefits.

Vermont's civil union statute provides for intestate succession of lesbian and gay Vermonters who registered a civil union. These couples are treated, under Vermont law, the same as a heterosexual married couple. The question

---

2. 42 U.S.C. §§ 401 *et seq.*

arises whether these same couples could apply for OASDI benefits under Title 42 of the United States Code.

The same issue is raised in California since that state also recognizes inheritance rights of domestic partners. The other twist of California law that makes it even more interesting is that heterosexuals over the age of sixty-two can enter into domestic partnerships as well. New Jersey's new domestic partner law also provides protection for heterosexual couples age sixty-two and older.

This is an untested theory. There is no case law on the issue and appears to be no law review articles on the subject. However, now that Massachusetts has begun to issue marriage licenses to same-sex couples the issue will become more imperative and legal challenges to any denial of benefits will take place.

This federal statute relies on the law of the insured's domicile to determine family status. Since state law controls, it would appear that a state that grants intestate inheritance rights to LG couples would also make those couples eligible for OASDI benefits under Title 42.

Medicaid and Medicare

Medicaid (Title XIX of the Social Security Act) is a federally funded, state-run program that provides medical assistance to low-income and low-resource individuals and families. General guidelines are established by the federal government; however, program requirements are set by the individual states.

Medicaid covers people in five broad categories:

- Children
- Pregnant women
- Adults in families with dependent children
- Individuals with disabilities
- Individuals age sixty-five and over

The states are responsible for establishing eligibility standards; type, amount, scope, and duration of services; rates of payment for services; and the administration of the program. State rules vary; eligibility in one state does not guarantee eligibility in another.

The states can also determine, to some extent, which services will be provided. One of the complications about Medicaid is that the rules can, and often do, change every year.

In addition to the federally funded Medicaid program, most states also have "state-only" programs to provide assistance to poor persons who do not qualify for Medicaid.

Lesbians and gay men who are age sixty-five and over are potentially eligible for Medicaid assistance. Lesbians and gay men under age sixty-five are potentially eligible *only* if they fall within one of the categories listed above.

In order to qualify for Medicaid for nursing home care, the client must spend down assets to a minimal amount. There is no consideration given to the needs of the other partner. The current amount ranges between $1,500 and $2,000. That represents the total amount of assets any individual Medicaid recipient can possess to qualify.

An individual's Social Security check will be turned over to the nursing home, although the resident will be allowed to keep a small amount for incidentals. This generally ranges from $25 to $50. The resident must dispose of all other assets. Any property sold for less than 80 percent of its fair market value may be viewed as an improper transfer. This determination can result in the applicant being deemed Medicaid ineligible for a specific period of time.

LG elders do not benefit from having a partner. Since same-sex marriages are not currently recognized, each partner will be considered an individual for Medicaid eligibility purposes.

Married couples can qualify for a community spouse payment. They are also eligible to keep their home even if titled in the name of the resident spouse. Similar consideration is not given to a same-sex couple.

Medicaid recipients may also be eligible for Medicare. Elderly lesbians and gay men are eligible to apply for Medicare once they reach age sixty-five. Dual eligibility usually comes into play with an elderly person when nursing home care becomes a factor.

Medicare will pay for skilled nursing care only. Medicare does not pay for custodial nursing home care. This can be a confusing topic to explain to a client. In a nutshell, medical conditions that require the services of a registered nurse, such as IVs or post-surgical care, usually qualify as skilled nursing care. Some nursing homes have skilled care wings on the property. Custodial care means the resident requires assistance with daily activities such as dressing, eating, and bathing. This type of care does not qualify for Medicare.

As mentioned earlier, an applicant for Medicaid must be impoverished to qualify for benefits. Some people try to create eligibility by transferring their property to others before submitting an application. That is why Medicaid created the look-back period. The usual look-back period is three years, although a five-year look-back period is in place for some transfers. This is a period of time during which any transfers will be deemed made in contemplation of applying for Medicaid. Mistakes in the transfer of assets to qualify for Medicaid may result in disqualification for a significant period of time. The applicant will be ineligible for Medicaid for a period of time equal to the value of the asset transferred.

Example: The applicant transferred a savings account of $15,000 to his partner a month before he applied. This transfer took the applicant's assets to $0. The nursing home costs $5,000 per month. Medicaid would deem the applicant ineligible for three months. This equals the amount of time the applicant would spend down the improperly transferred asset—three months at $5,000 per month.

Some people plan their estate to cover up to three years of nursing home care and transfer their other assets when they enter the nursing home. If the individual can pay for the nursing home care for the duration of the look-back period, the transfer will be valid.

Example: The resident transfers his only asset, the house, to his partner two years before entering the nursing home. The fair market value of the house is $100,000. The annual cost of the nursing home is $40,000. The resident will be ineligible for Medicaid for one year and will be required to pay for his care during that time. After that one year—three years after the transfer—he will become eligible for Medicaid.

Medicaid also does not cover all expenses. In some cases a Medicaid, or special needs, trust may be appropriate, particularly in situations where one or both partners suffer from a life-threatening disease such as AIDS. In those situations, it is necessary to research your state law to determine the types of special needs trusts that are available and how to draft them to protect your clients. It may be necessary to draft special needs trusts for both partners. For example, a special needs trust may be established to provide for a Medicaid recipient's needs not covered by the program.

There are different types of trusts available. The state permits these trusts because it will recover its costs upon the death of the recipient. In some cases the state recovers its expenses up to 50 percent of the remaining trust res, and in others the entire balance is turned over to the state. This does not protect the individual's heirs but can provide a more comfortable life for the Medicaid recipient.

Medicaid is a complicated program and it helps to consult with someone well versed in its intricacies. The state's Long-Term Care Ombudsman office can be very helpful in deciphering the Medicaid rules.

There are also tax consequences. The gift tax issue is discussed in Chapter 4.

If the Medicaid recipient has community assets that were not counted when determining eligibility, the state may place a lien on that property. The state then enforces the lien after the resident dies to recover the cost of care. This can occur if the resident and his partner jointly owned a house and the resident's name remained on the house. The state's lien would continue until the house was sold. The state could then recover at least a portion of the sale price.

This is another instance where contributions to the purchase of the house and its upkeep are vitally important. If the resident partner cannot prove he contributed to the purchase of the house, the state may argue that the value of the house belonged solely to the Medicaid recipient.

Life insurance can help counter recovery efforts by Medicaid against the estate of a deceased recipient. Proceeds from the insurance policy may be needed to pay off Medicaid if the state attempts to recover the cost of care from the decedent's estate. The couple may want to take out life insurance on each other for contingencies such as this.

Medicaid is a tricky subject and the states are cutting back on benefits. It is welfare, and recipients must be poor. The states will continue to enact laws and regulations that afford them the opportunity to recover outlays from the recipient's estate.

In situations involving same-sex couples, documentation concerning joint accounts will be even more important. It is likely that states will demand proof of actual joint ownership and contribution when making Medicaid eligibility determinations. Many times your clients will not have extensive documentation about who contributed what to where, but it is necessary to recreate the documentation if possible or start from that point forward. Such documentation will also serve the couple well when dealing with the Internal Revenue Service.

Insurance Concerns of Lesbian and Gay Seniors

It is important for LG seniors to consider their need for various types of insurance. This includes long-term care insurance, disability insurance, and life insurance.

The long-term care insurance should include coverage for in-home and nursing home care. A client may be more comfortable knowing he can remain in his home with proper care and avoid the potential pitfalls of being gay in a heterosexual nursing home.

Life insurance can relieve the couple's concern about the ability of the surviving partner to remain in the home.

Disability insurance can provide a welcome cushion in the event one partner becomes ill and is no longer able to work. The most cost-effective policies come through professional groups or organizations. A policy that waives premiums at a certain point is also beneficial to the couple.

Most lesbians and gay men do not have employers who provide health insurance for domestic partners. Health insurance is an enormous and expensive problem in this country, and lesbians and gay men are not immune. It is important to ascertain whether the clients have health insurance.

Medical expenses are often a reason for bankruptcy filing. Example: If the couple does not own their home jointly and the titleholder becomes ill, the house may be jeopardized. If the titleholder's health deteriorates to the point where he must enter a nursing home, the house is a countable resource for Medicaid eligibility determination. In a same-sex couple, the needs of the resident's partner are not considered.

Likewise, if the titleholder incurs a catastrophic illness, the house is vulnerable to his creditors for payment of outstanding medical bills. Unlike married heterosexual couples, same-sex couples have no spousal rights to the "manor house."

Life insurance can benefit the surviving partner in the tax arena. Unlike married couples, same-sex couples have no exemption from property tax reassessment at the death of one partner. Transferring property from joint ownership to a sole owner can cause a reassessment of property taxes. The surviving partner may be unable to pay the increased taxes and that places the house at risk. Life insurance can alleviate this concern and provide sufficient funds to pay the property tax increase.

As has been stated, the IRS presumes that the first person to die owned all the jointly held property. The parties must rebut the agency's position through extensive records, including receipts and tax returns.

Conclusion

The needs of LG seniors mirror, in many cases, those of the rest of the senior population. There are lesbian and gay retirement communities cropping up around the country. However, most lesbians and gay men have lived in mixed communities all their lives. Not everyone wants to enter a community comprised mostly of lesbians or gay men.

Sexual orientation is not a determinative factor when discussing health care, long-term care, or alternative living arrangements. Most people want to remain in their homes. Many of us will require additional assistance as we age. Many LG persons do not have an extended family unit. Often their families are comprised of other persons in the gay community.

Taxes paid by LG seniors entitle them to the same benefits that hetero-sexual seniors receive. There can be no differentiation between seniors based on sexual orientation. This is an untested field of law, however; extensive litigation may be necessary to ensure fair and equitable treatment for all seniors without regard to sexual orientation. The *Lawrence* decision may be the foundation for arguments to protect the rights of LG senior Americans.

Chapter 9

Other Issues and Considerations

Dealing with same-sex couples in life or estate planning situations presents issues and considerations that do not occur with heterosexual married couples. Opposite-sex unmarried couples also have the option of marrying, which places them in a different position from same-sex couples.

This chapter will address some of the issues that you need to consider when advising lesbian and gay (LG) individuals and couples. This is an evolving area of law and it is possible that changes will occur in time. The issues to be addressed include Medicare and Medicaid, Social Security benefits, and private and government retirement accounts.

Debts, Credit Reports, and Credit Cards

In 2003, Congress enacted amendments to the Fair Credit Reporting Act (FCRA).[1] The Fair and Accurate Credit Transactions Act of 2003 (FACTA)[2] expands consumer rights in the credit area.

There are different provisions in FACTA and their effective dates vary. Practitioners must research the client's credit issues to determine whether any of the new amendments apply. Of particular importance is the free credit report. Credit reporting agencies are required to provide a free annual report upon the consumer's request. The Federal Trade Commission issued the Final Rule on Free Annual Credit Reports on June 4, 2004.[3]

Credit Reports

Many LG couples have joint accounts and joint debts. It is important for clients to check their credit reports annually. There are three national credit-reporting

---

1. 15 U.S.C.A. §§ 1681 *et seq.*
2. Pub. L. No. 108-159 (Dec. 4, 2003).
3. C.F.R. pts 610, 698.

Credit Reporting Agencies

TransUnion Corporation
Consumer Disclosure Center
P. O. Box 2000
Chester, PA 19022
800-916-8800
Order Credit Report: (800) 888-4213
http://www.transunion.com
Cost: $9.00*

Experian
Consumer Assistance
P. O. Box 2104
Allen, TX 75013
(888) 397-3742
http://www.experian.com
Cost: $9.00*

Equifax
Consumer Department
P. O. Box 740241
Atlanta, GA 30374-0241
(800) 685-1111
http://www.equifax.com
Cost: $9.00*

Information needed:
- Name
- Current address
- Social Security number
- Date of birth

* Some state laws provide for an annual free credit report. A new provision of the Fair Credit Reporting Act will also require credit reporting agencies to provide annual free reports to consumers.

agencies (Experian, Equifax, and TransUnion) that collect credit information on individuals. (See box above.) Your clients do not need to get a credit report from each credit-reporting agency. It is usually sufficient to get a copy from the nearest company. Each agency has a Web site from which a report can be requested.

Some of the joint accounts and debts may be from previous relationships. It is advisable to check the reports to ensure that these accounts and debts are no longer active. Part of the estate plan will be to clear up loose ends from prior relationships.

Checking a credit report will also reveal if the credit reporting agency is intermingling the parties' credit histories. This is more common than most people realize. It is important to correct the report because inaccurate information will wreak havoc on an individual's ability to obtain credit. It can also adversely affect a person's employment status. The federal Fair Credit Reporting Act entitles your client to check her credit report and demand that corrections be made. The credit-reporting agency is required by the FCRA to correct the report and remove false or outdated information. If after an investigation the item remains disputed, your client has the right to include a statement about the situation and explain her position.

Unlike heterosexual couples, gay and lesbian couples do not have the option of going into domestic relations court. While state contract law can govern the relationships, most gay men and lesbians do not use the courts to resolve differences when breakups occur.

Same-sex couples often seek joint credit accounts. This can be in the form of a mortgage, credit cards, and the like. Because credit issuers are interested in extending credit, discrimination on the basis of sexual orientation is not common.

However, if a client believes a credit issuer denied credit because of the applicant's sexual orientation, there is little protection. There may be a local or state law that applies but that is as far as it goes. The Equal Credit Opportunity Act does not include sexual orientation as a prohibited basis for denying credit. There are no court decisions that extend coverage of the act to sexual orientation.

Credit Accounts

Getting credit today is easy. Getting joint credit is, in some cases, even easier. As long as one applicant has sufficient income to qualify as a good credit risk, a credit card will be issued.

Both parties on the account have the ability to use the card. Both parties are equally liable for the balance. This is one of the few times a commercial enterprise will treat a same-sex couple as "family." However, it is important to advise your clients that they should not list themselves as spouses, no matter how long they have been together. The term "spouse" is a legal term of art and carries specific obligations concerning liability and responsibility. Applying as "spouses" could subject your clients to a charge of fraud because they lied on the application.

Tax Returns

Same-sex couples cannot file joint federal tax returns. This will not change anytime soon. The Vermont civil union statute, while permitting couples to file joint state tax returns, does not alter this fact. The situation may become less clear now that Massachusetts has begun issuing civil marriage licenses to same-sex couples. If those couples challenge the federal Defense of Marriage Act, constitutional issues under equal protection will be raised.

If one partner is providing financial support for the other, it is possible to file a single return and name the partner as a "dependent." There are requirements to qualify in this regard: The dependent must be an unmarried person, be a United States citizen, and have gross income under $2,900; the support provided must be at least 50 percent of the total annual support; the person must have lived in the filer's home for a full year; and the relationship must not violate local law. That last requirement is open to debate since there is no guidance from the Internal Revenue Service as to its meaning.

Filing as a head of household is also an option, especially when children are present or if one partner provides over 50 percent of the other's support. The IRS may object to this classification. The client needs to be prepared to defend the classification with documentation.

Social Security Benefits

As a federal program, the Social Security Act does not recognize same-sex relationships. The Defense of Marriage Act explicitly precludes coverage. Each member of a same-sex couple is entitled only to her individual Social Security account. There is no eligibility for "spousal" benefits or survivor benefits. The nonbiological children of one partner are not entitled to receive any benefits upon the death of that partner even if she was their primary or sole support. In states that do not permit second-parent or joint adoptions, the children pay the price.

Same-sex couples do not benefit from the federal guarantee of payments to a surviving spouse, former spouse, unmarried children, or children disabled before age twenty-two. There is also no entitlement to the $255 death payment that goes to the surviving spouse or children. Individual gay or lesbian clients may have other dependents that can be deemed eligible. These include grandchildren, great-grandchildren, and dependent parents.

In situations like that clients may want to purchase life insurance in order to protect the children. Each partner will need to purchase her own policy because insurance companies do not recognize any "insurable interest" between the partners. Some people state there is a "business relationship" in order to purchase a policy on the life of another. Spouses, business partners, and joint homeowners have insurable interests that can be protected.

Medicare is another area that is limited to an individual. Same-sex couples do not qualify for any joint benefits under Medicare.

Pension and Retirement Plans

There are different pension and retirement plans available today. The types, allowable contribution limits, and rules change often enough to require a lawyer to take action to keep current.

The issue of retirement benefits is difficult for LG couples. Many plans expressly provide that only surviving spouses or children are eligible for survivor benefits. Think of the Tampa, Florida, police officer. LG couples can take some steps when addressing the issue of retirement plans. Clients need to review their employers' plans and look for any restrictions on naming beneficiaries. Clients should consider taking advantage of IRAs or other types of retirement vehicles. Clients may also consider retirement plans as a vehicle for charitable bequests. This option can result in no tax, income or estate.

Individual Retirement Accounts, both traditional and Roth, are in vogue and serve the needs of a variety of people. The proceeds from these plans go to the named beneficiary, outside of probate. It is important to ensure that your clients have named the beneficiary on these plans. Failure to do so places the proceeds into the estate and subject to probate. There are no laws that preclude same-sex partners from naming each other as the beneficiary.

The same is true for 401(k) plans. The employee has the option of designating a beneficiary to receive the proceeds upon his death. The only restriction applies to married employees. The surviving spouse must be named as the beneficiary unless the spouse waives that right.

The federal government offers a Thrift Savings Plan (TSP) for employees. This is primarily for those employees covered under the Federal Employees Retirement System (FERS). This system replaced the Civil Service Retirement System (CSRS) that covered federal employees for eons.

The TSP program is comparable to a 401(k) plan. The employees can contribute up to the maximum amount and the government contributes up to 5 percent. The employee can name a beneficiary to receive the proceeds upon death. There is a question as to whether the government's contribution will be included in the dispersal of the funds.

Employees enrolled in the CSRS program can also contribute to the TSP plan but their contributions are limited and there is no government contribution.

Active-duty military personnel can also participate in the TSP program. This is in addition to any retirement benefits the service member may be eligible for upon retirement. Military personnel can retire after twenty years of active duty. Military reservists are eligible to retire after compiling a sufficient number of points and reaching the age of sixty-two.

Under CSRS, employees do not pay Social Security taxes. Employees receive an annuity upon retirement. If the retiree is also eligible for Social Security payments there is a dollar-for-dollar reduction from the annuity. There is no provision for nonspouses to receive a portion of the retiree's CSRS benefits. The retiree may elect to reduce the annuity in order to provide for a surviving-spouse annuity. However, this does not apply to same-sex couples.

Federal employees who will retire under CSRS are also eligible to set up a TSP account and can name a partner as the beneficiary of the TSP proceeds.

Clients who are federal employees will be better off taking the full amount of the annuity and investing it. The retiree's partner will not be able to file a claim for survivor benefits unless Congress changes the law.

Federal employees enrolled in the FERS program cannot name a same-sex partner as a surviving annuitant. They can, however, name their partner as the beneficiary of the TSP account.

The TSP account can also be rolled over into an IRA in the same manner as a 401(k) when the federal employee leaves government service.

Pensions are different from an IRA. The Employee Retirement Income Security Act (ERISA) controls company pensions. If your client is eligible to participate in an employer's pension plan be sure to get a copy of the summary plan description, a summary annual report, and information on survivor/ beneficiary coverage.

Some plans offer a lump-sum payment. For same-sex couples this is the best way to get control of the retirement funds. By removing them from the employer's control, the retiree can then name anyone she wishes as benefici-ary. This may be particularly important for federal employees. Rolling over the TSP account into an IRA through an outside brokerage will include all contributions. Once the rollover is complete the retiree or former employee has complete control over the funds. This is beneficial to same-sex couples because any restrictive rules applied by the former employer no longer apply.

Military Retired Pay

Military retired pay is an entitlement program and not a retirement plan or a pension plan. There is no entitlement to military retired pay until the service member completes twenty years of active duty or accumulates the required number of points for reserve duty.

There is no accrued value or vested interest while the member is serving. Also, while military retired pay is subject to division in a divorce or dissolu-tion, only spouses are eligible to apply for a portion of a member's military retired pay. The Uniformed Services Former Spouse's Protection Act[4] governs the division of military retired pay. The civilian partner in a same-sex couple has absolutely and unequivocally no right to military retired pay.

In addition, a veteran has no ability to provide for a same-sex partner from veteran's benefits.

---

4. 10 U.S.C. §§ 1408, *et seq.*

Nursing Homes, Retirement Communities, and Home Health Care

There is very little research available on discrimination against gay and lesbian elders in long-term care facilities, home health care, or retirement communities. There is anecdotal evidence that discrimination does occur.

In some cases, long-time couples are prevented from sharing a "couple's room" or associating with each other. Some nursing homes have been known to deny the nonresident partner access to the resident partner. Some gay men and lesbians have returned to the closet when entering a nursing home because it is safer.

There are no laws that prevent discrimination in these situations. As with society in general, no one, including the gay community, is addressing the unique needs of LG elders.

Discriminatory treatment of LG elders may become a source of litigation in the near future. There has been a rash of nursing home litigation going on throughout the country. Several states are considering legislation that will prohibit such litigation—all at the urging of the nursing home industry.

Home health care companies are also seen as a possible source of abuse and discriminatory activities. There is one report of an abusive home health care aide who threatened to "out" the elderly patient if he complained about her actions.

It is important to remember that many elderly gay men and lesbians are not as "public" as their younger counterparts. They grew up in an age that is quite different from what we experience now. Sodomy and anti-gay statutes were rampant as was enforcement. These people were very private about their relationships. It is not unusual to find couples in a fifty-year relationship refer to each other as "my friend." It reflects the accepted euphemism for a gay relationship.

Because of the lack of antidiscrimination laws there is no guarantee that elderly LG clients will not be subjected to abuse in situations designed to help them. In fact, it is possible the courts will find no cause of action if the facility's acts are based on the individual's sexual orientation. It will be necessary to have a back-up cause of action to keep the case in court.

Assisted living facilities are, for the most part, unregulated hotels. Neither Medicare nor Medicaid rules govern their operation. These are privately run facilities operated by for-profit companies. In some respects, it may be easier for gay or lesbian seniors to be treated well so long as they can pay for the services. However, because these facilities are not regulated, there will be an increasing number of problems coming to light. This is particularly true in the area of dispensing medications. Many assisted living facilities are not equipped to dispense medications. There is no registered nurse on duty and no law requiring one to be present. This is a potential disaster waiting to happen.

There are retirement communities in place and more being planned for LG seniors. The problem is that most of them require the senior to be in good health and to be relatively well off financially. This excludes a significant segment of the LG elder population.

The sexual orientation of nursing home residents is not yet on the radar screen. Most people do not start considering nursing homes until a crisis occurs and there is no other choice.

Attorneys may want to develop a referral list for their gay and lesbian clients to consider if a nursing home or home health care becomes necessary. Identifying those facilities that treat everyone with dignity and respect will benefit not only your LG clients but heterosexual clients as well.

Foreign Same-Sex Marriages, Religious Same-Sex Marriages, and Civil Unions

As of this writing, Vermont is the only state that recognizes civil unions. The Vermont law has been in effect since July 1, 2000.

There is no residency requirement to enter into a civil union in Vermont. Couples need a license from the town clerk and a ceremony conducted by a clergy member, a judge, or a justice of the peace. Residency is required to dissolve a civil union in the Vermont courts.

Hundreds of ceremonies have taken place since the enactment of the law. Many of the ceremonies involved non-Vermonters. No other state has, as yet, recognized a Vermont civil union. Some states are passing legislation that explicitly prohibits recognition of these unions.

There will come a time, however, when someone will challenge these prohibitions. Vermont civil unions may not be among the first cases because there is another avenue available.

Some foreign countries are recognizing gay marriages. American citizens who marry in a foreign country want their marriages recognized by their home state. That is fact. The question will be raised when an American gay couple, married in a foreign country that sanctions gay marriage, returns to the United States and seeks the rights of a married couple under civil law. The full faith and credit clause of the U.S. Constitution, and its application to the states, will be an integral part of any litigation.

Canada has announced that same-sex marriage will be recognized in that country. Toronto is issuing marriage licenses for same-sex couples, many of whom come from the United States.

Massachusetts began issuing marriage licenses to same-sex couples in May 2004. Even if a constitutional amendment (state or federal) passes at some future date, there will be same-sex couples who have a valid, legal civil marriage in Massachusetts. Will lesbian and gay couples married in Massachusetts be entitled to have their marriages recognized in other states under the full faith and credit clause of the Constitution? That question has not been answered. But there is currently a movement afoot to amend the Constitution to provide that marriage is between a man and a woman.

Another interesting issue involves churches whose teachings recognize same-sex marriages. So far, there has been a religious argument against same-sex marriages. What happens when a church, through its teachings, recognizes, supports, and encourages same-sex marriages? Do we then enter into a discussion as to whose church's teachings are acceptable? What are the First Amendment issues? This is a question that has not been raised to date. The courts have ruled on religious teachings in the past and found them contrary to secular laws. Examples include the use of peyote in Native American rites and polygamy as practiced by the Mormons. If the federal Constitution is amended to recognize only heterosexual marriages, will that amendment inherently conflict with the First Amendment, or with the Fourteenth Amendment?

Lawsuits are filed because a county clerk will not issue a marriage license. Is a marriage license mandatory to establish a valid marriage? New York courts have ruled they are not.

In 2000, a New York trial court[5] found that a valid marriage existed even though the state never issued a license. A couple exchanged promises during a religious service. More than one hundred guests attended the ceremony. This involved a Hindu prayer ceremony and was sufficient to make the couple husband and wife. The court held, "[T]here is an old cliché that goes, 'if it walks like a duck and quacks like a duck and looks like a duck, it's a duck.' This familiar maxim appears perfectly suited to the case at bar, as it conforms with the intent underlying the statutory construction enacted by the legislature. Essentially, the Domestic Relations law establishes that where parties participate in a solemn marriage ceremony officiated by a clergyman

---

5. Persad v. Balram, 187 Misc. 2d 711 (Sup. Ct. Queens Cty. 2001).

or magistrate wherein they exchange vows, they are married in the eyes of the law."

Another New York case in 2002 came to the same conclusion.[6]

Business Succession

Part of the estate planning process requires that you determine if the parties are in business together. Determine the type of business and what form it takes. Determine if the client is in a business relationship with anyone else and what form that arrangement takes. Are there written agreements?

The primary areas of concern in business estate planning are the operation of the business after death, estate tax concerns, and probate avoidance.

Does the client have a buy-sell agreement concerning the business? Are family members involved? Is it a family-owned and -operated business that restricts the disposition of any one person's interest on death? Is there a "right of first refusal" agreement between co-owners? What happens if the other owners do not buy out the decedent's interest?

The client should be advised to obtain a business valuation by an objective outside appraiser. This will help refute an IRS evaluation.

Business succession planning is also important. Review the client's organizational documents and make sure they coordinate with the estate plan you are developing.

Successful planning is dependent on a number of factors. These include the relationship between the current and future owners, cash sources, and how the parties deal with each other on an emotional, personal level. It is important to identify and resolve latent, unresolved problem areas that may mushroom in the future.

Long-Term Care Insurance

Long-term care insurance is a valuable planning tool for LG clients. These policies cover home health care, nursing home care, and physical therapy. Depending on the policy, other matters may also be covered. The insurance protects the insured against unplanned costs.

This type of insurance is best if purchased at a young age when the insured is in good health. It is important to find a flexible plan that provides for different care options. Clients need to consider whether the policy pro-

---

6. Ramyard v. Ali, No. 21297/2002 (Sup. Ct. Queens Cty. 2002).

vides for inflation indexing of the benefits provided. Premiums vary and are based on duration and the type of coverage selected. Some companies, such as American Express Financial, offer joint policies for same-sex couples that can be more cost effective than individual policies.

Many younger LG clients may question the need for such coverage. This is an opportunity to discuss the potential costs involved in caring for someone with a catastrophic illness or injury. Also, long-term care insurance can offset the restricted coverage under Medicaid. LG couples are considered individuals when determining Medicaid eligibility and can have no more than $1,500 to $2,000 in assets to qualify.

Generally, premiums remain constant during the life of the coverage. It may be a small price to pay for peace of mind.

Disability Insurance

LG individuals and couples need to protect themselves every step of the way. Disability insurance is another necessary topic for discussion during the estate planning process. The disability plan should provide for payments if the insured is unable to perform her current job. Otherwise, she may be denied coverage if there is a job she could do, even one for which she is unqualified.

Group plans offered by employers or professional organizations usually carry the lowest premiums. Individual plans can be cost prohibitive. Still, disability insurance is essential because there is no guarantee there will be any other source of income.

If the insured pays his own premiums, any payments received are nontaxable. Payments received from an employer-paid plan are taxable to the recipient.

Conclusion

Any lawyer representing LG clients, either individuals or couples, will be challenged to provide creative and encompassing legal assistance. The issues faced by gay men and lesbians are in some ways becoming simpler and in others more complex. The answers are far from easy. And it is up to you, as the lawyer, to recognize potential problems and pitfalls.

This is an exciting area of practice. The rules are changing quickly. What is true one day is altered the next. Practicing in this area requires patience, tenacity, creativity, and open-mindedness in order to properly serve the needs of the lesbian or gay client.

Chapter 10

Finding and Marketing to the Gay Community

Unlike many other groups, it takes a bit of effort to market to the lesbian and gay (LG) community. The community includes gay men, lesbians, bisexuals, and transgendered persons.

Due to the discrimination and violence experienced by members of the gay community over the years, many people keep their sexual orientation quiet. While a growing number of gays and lesbians are openly gay, a large number of people have not yet reached that decision.

Any lawyer representing or providing services to members of the gay community needs to consider these issues. You may find yourself representing a client who does not want anyone to know about his or her sexual orientation. The fear is well founded. All you have to do is read the newspaper to learn of the discrimination your client faces.

As a lawyer representing LG clients, you must also be prepared for the question, "Are you gay?" One Cleveland lawyer discovered this after giving a presentation at a continuing legal education (CLE) seminar on estate issues affecting same-sex couples. The rumor started and she was amazed at the reaction of some of her colleagues. She then came to a better understanding of what clients endure on a daily basis.

Marketing to the LG community, while requiring particular creativity and sensitivity, is no different from any other marketing plan. Many gays and lesbians may be suspicious of straight persons who "want to help." Still, the members of this community need the legal services you can provide.

You need not go to gay bars to find clients. In fact, you can begin by telling family and friends that you are seeking lesbian and gay clients.

The following are possible sources of referrals:

- Friends and relatives
- Other lawyers
- Current and former clients
- Life insurance agents
- Financial planners
- Bankers
- Accountants
- Law schools
- Attorney referral services
- School alumni groups

Have a Plan

As with any marketing proposal it is important to have a plan, a goal; set a benchmark against which to evaluate the success of the endeavor. In some areas of this country, openly marketing to the gay community may be unpleasant. While the 2000 census clearly establishes that there are millions of same-sex households in this country, it is more likely you will find a viable LG community in a metropolitan area.

Drafting a business plan with a comprehensive marketing strategy is one way to investigate the advantages and disadvantages of providing services to the LG community. There are more potential clients than there are attorneys available to serve them.

The estate-planning arena provides the most promise for incursion into this client base. As with the rest of the population, LG boomers are growing older and need to make estate-planning arrangements. The time is ripe to develop and implement a marketing strategy that puts your name and expertise in front of this client base. Be prepared to throw the net out wide. The experience will be professionally and personally satisfying.

As part of a strategic marketing plan, you must

- Develop a mission statement that includes your core beliefs, the purpose of your practice, and your vision of the practice of law
- Define the services to be offered
- Identify your targeted audience (lesbians, gay men, both)
- Define your referral sources (current clients, word of mouth, etc.)
- Describe the offered services in the marketing materials
- Train your staff to present the services to the targeted clients

Marketing Books

James A. Durham and Deborah McMurray, eds., *The Lawyer's Guide to Marketing Your Practice,* 2d ed. (American Bar Association, 2004)

Theda C. Snyder, *Women Rainmakers' Best Marketing Tips,* 2d ed. (American Bar Association, 2003)

Gregory H. Siskind, Deborah McMurray, & Richard P. Klau, *The Lawyer's Guide to Marketing on the Internet,* 2d ed. (American Bar Association, 2002)

William E. Hornsby, Jr., *Marketing and Legal Ethics: The Boundaries of Promoting Legal Services,* 3d ed. (American Bar Association, 2000)

Milton Zwicker, *Successful Client Newsletters: The Complete Guide to Creating Powerful Newsletters* (American Bar Association, 1998)

Appendix B lists a variety of resources available to you when planning your marketing strategy.

Marketing to a Niche

The gay community is a niche practice market. The mantra in real estate is location, location, location. In marketing, it is focus, focus, focus. Marketing is more effective when directed toward a targeted audience. Develop and write down your strategic marketing plan. Define your target audience. This allows you to focus your marketing efforts. As part of your marketing strategy, determine the relevant benefits you offer and how they appeal to the target audience. Your plan must incorporate developing contact strategies and devising a media plan, including direct marketing and detailed advertising copy. This allows you to determine in advance what you want to accomplish and the steps you need to take to realize your goal.

Including your staff in developing any strategic marketing plan is essential, particularly for solo practitioners and small firms. Your staff can build consensus concerning the focus of a marketing plan. A professional, well-trained staff makes the marketing effort more productive because clients see these people first.

Equip your staff with their own business cards and encourage them to hand them out. Set out generic cards, containing your practice areas, in the reception area.

Focus groups can be one way to determine where and how to spend your marketing resources in the LG community. This type of research helps you build your distinctive brand in the LG community.

The legal problems facing LG clients are not all gay-related. All clients want an attorney in whom they can confide and with whom they feel comfortable. Being able to discuss freely their relationship, the effect the legal problem has on that relationship, and how best to resolve it, is the cornerstone of attorney-client interactions. It is particularly so for LG clients.

At the same time, the client's sexual orientation may be germane to many legal issues. The client's sexual orientation may take main stage in family law matters, such as custody, support, visitation, and adoption. Being able to talk to a sympathetic lawyer can make all the difference in the world. Word will get out and your client base will grow.

Marketing efforts also include becoming involved in the clients' community. The Lesbian and Gay Community Centers have a board of directors that may need legal assistance. Offering to provide services, on a pro bono or reduced-fee basis, to a nonprofit organization can serve as an introduction to the community. Serving on the board is another way to make yourself known to the community.

Lesbian and gay groups are not limited to the local community centers. You can also approach the local branch of AIDS Task Force and offer to take referrals. Advertise in that organization's publication and offer a discount on a specific service. The staff at these organizations can also benefit from your information and assistance and are another source of potential clients. The staff can also arrange a seminar for their clients.

People who are HIV positive or diagnosed with AIDS face many different legal issues, including estate planning. These people often have limited funds to pay for an attorney's assistance. However, it does not mean you are looking at pro bono work. You may make lower fees but you will gain a reputation for providing superior legal services and, as a result, find more clients.

The local gay newspaper is another source of potential clients. Identify the financial planners, insurance agents, and other professionals who advertise there. Include them on your mailing list for a newsletter on legal issues targeted to the LG community.

The local gay newspaper will also include information on various LG organizations operating in your area. Becoming a member of the groups that interest you is another way to network in the LG community. For example, many cities have LG dinner groups that meet monthly at a local restaurant. These groups include speakers in their monthly meetings and this is a marketing option available to you.

There are newspapers and magazines that cater to the LG community on the local and national level. These publications carry advertisements for

Internet Listings of Lesbian and Gay Publications

Gay Media Database: http://www.gaydata.com

Queer Information Network:

   http://www.manifestonews.org/QIN/publications/index.html (publications listings, by state and city, with links)

Gay and Lesbian Organizations and Publications:

   http://www.faculty.Washington.edu/alvin/gayorg.htm (nonprofit and information-providing organizations)

National Lesbian and Gay Publications

The Advocate: http://www.advocate.com

Girlfriends: http://www.girlfriendsmag.com

Curve: http://www.curvemag.com

Out: http://www.out.com

Poz, targeting health issues of persons who are HIV positive and persons with AIDS: http://www.poz.com

Alternative Family, an international parenting magazine: http://www.altfammag.com

Gay Parenting Magazine: http://www.gayparentmag.com

Passport Magazine: http://www.passportmagazine.net

Cybersocket Web Magazine: http://www.cybersocket.com

Instinct Magazine, gay male lifestyle: http://www.instinctmag.com

QV Magazine, gay Latino men's magazine: http://www.qvmagazine.com

Genre Magazine, upscale gay male magazine: http://www.genremagazine.com

Art & Understanding, national AIDS magazine: http://www.aumag.org

professional services. This is another way to maximize your marketing efforts to a specific community. Many gay men and lesbians do not know how to find a lawyer and these resources should not be overlooked.

Lesbian and Gay Legal Organizations

The National Lesbian and Gay Law Association (NLGLA) is a national association of lawyers, judges, and other legal professionals. Every year the NLGLA hosts a national conference, "Lavender Law," involving attorneys from across the country. Membership dues are based on a sliding scale depending on income. NLGLA is an affiliate of the American Bar Association and sponsors CLE sessions at the ABA Annual and Midyear meetings. The organization is also represented in the ABA's House of Delegates.

The Lambda Legal Defense and Education Fund (Lambda) is the premier organization providing legal assistance to members of the LG community. Most of their work revolves around significant groundbreaking legal issues. Lambda represented the appellants in the precedent-setting U.S. Supreme Court case of *Lawrence v. Texas,*[1] decided by the Court in June 2003.

Lambda also assists private attorneys dealing with lesbian and gay issues. The organization seeks out volunteer lawyers to assist in their advocacy efforts. Lambda has offices in New York, Los Angeles, Chicago, and Atlanta. Lambda actively encourages lawyers to join their attorney referral list. This puts you in a position to advertise your affiliation with one of the leading LG legal organizations in the United States.

The National Center for Lesbian Rights (NCLR) provides legal assistance to the lesbian community. The NCLR successfully represented Sharon Smith, the surviving partner of Diane Whipple. A neighbor's dogs killed Ms. Whipple in the hallway outside her apartment. The NCLR succeeded in winning a court decision giving standing to Ms. Smith to bring a wrongful death action.

Like Lambda, the NCLR maintains a list of private lawyers to whom prospective clients can be referred. These referrals can be fee generating or pro bono.

The key is that lesbians and gay men look to these organizations to locate attorneys who are interested in representing them. They seek attorneys who are familiar with the needs of a gay man or lesbian and who will treat them with respect.

While this book deals with estate planning issues affecting members of the gay community, referrals from these organizations can also be in other areas of the law. There is no need to limit your practice to estate planning. Once the word gets out about an attorney representing gays and lesbians, you will find that these are clients with problems like anyone else. At that point, their sexual orientation will be a nonissue between you and your client.

Educational Seminars

Public speaking is another way to develop a client base and establish you as a person experienced with LG issues. Seminars on issues of importance to the

---

1. Lawrence v. Texas, 539 U.S. 558, 123 S. CT. 2472, 156 L.Ed.2d 508, 2003 U.S. LEXIS 5013 (June 26, 2003).

gay community are an effective marketing tool. They are focused on the targeted audience. Estate planning is a natural way to encourage people to come to the seminar. Use this hook to persuade people to attend.

Most estate-planning seminars fail to address the needs of same-sex couples because the presenters do not think about it. Yet many lesbians and gay men attend these seminars hoping to glean some information about their unique situation.

Estate planning, combined with responsible financial planning, is becoming more of an issue in the LG community. American Express Financial Advisors and Prudential Securities regularly present seminars for the LG community. Presenting a joint seminar with these financial planners provides an opportunity for an entrepreneurial attorney to expand her client base. However, keep in mind any multidisciplinary practice rules in your jurisdiction.

Contact the local Lesbian and Gay Community Center to arrange a seminar there. Advertising in the center's newsletter or on its Web site will be easy. The center's staff is usually willing to assist in identifying the best way to advertise the event. Further, it puts you in a good position to advertise your professional services to a targeted audience.

Provide handouts, with your contact information, that include tips on obtaining legal protection in a same-sex relationship. Point out how the law does not always apply to a same-sex relationship. The intestate laws alone are often enough to get people to sit up and take notice.

Offer to write a column in the local gay newspaper on legal issues. Take questions and provide feedback. Most gay newspapers do not have this type of column and it will be of great interest to the readers.

Other seminar presentation opportunities include

- Adult education seminars
- Church groups
- LG social groups
- LG senior groups
- Professional organizations
- School alumni groups
- Local colleges and universities

Write a Newsletter

Newsletters are your opportunity to talk to clients, current and prospective, about yourself, your practice, and legal issues of interest to them. Newsletters need not be fancy. Include basic information about estate planning. Topics such as wills, trusts, and hospital visitation are of interest to the lesbian and gay community. Explain why it is necessary to prepare an estate plan even if the "estate" consists only of clothing and CDs. Include a discussion of the intestate succession laws in your state.

Hot topics in the lesbian and gay arena include adoptions, property rights, tort rights, employment discrimination, hospital visitation, and family law issues. Since the *Lawrence* decision, there is a growing interest in the possibility of same-sex marriage in the United States. This is a time to talk about your state's laws, how they affect the client, and whether there is a state Defense of Marriage Act.

The area of law affecting equal rights for the gay community is changing rapidly. Your newsletter can address changes in the law on a national and state level. This includes changes in other states and how those changes affect the actions taken by your clients in their home state. The newsletter can include a list of the services you offer.

The newsletter need not be long; two to four pages are sufficient. Word processing programs make preparing newsletters easier than ever. Write in a straightforward manner; forget the legalese and use plain English.

The newsletter can also take an e-format. E-mail addresses should be part of the information you obtain from all clients. To avoid problems, ask if the client wants to receive your e-newsletter. The electronic format is also cheaper to produce and can be updated quickly.

It is possible to retain the services of a freelance writer to ghostwrite the newsletter for you. This is particularly helpful for those attorneys who have neither the interest nor the skills to be the next John Grisham. You provide the content and the writer will put it into readable prose. To avoid the cost of a freelance writer, you may offer the writing opportunity to a qualified member of your staff. Your goal is to create a readable, well-written newsletter that promotes you and your practice.

One format that is particularly suitable in a newsletter is the FAQ: frequently asked questions. Your regular newsletter can address different FAQs each time you publish.

The newsletter can be printed and folded at the local copy center. You may be able to barter your services for those of the printer. The newsletter can be distributed by mail or by dropping off copies at locations frequented by the LG community. The LG Community Centers are always good places to leave materials. Ask about having the newsletter included in the center's next mailing. Offer to cover part of the cost.

Newsletters can be useful when marketing to a new client base. You can learn more about the process with Milton W. Zwicker's book, *Successful Client Newsletters: The Complete Guide to Creating Powerful Newsletters* (see "Marketing Books" box on page 109).

The newsletters, both electronic and paper, can later be used to create short pamphlets for your clients. These pamphlets, on specific issues such as wills, trusts, probate, and consumer rights, can also be left at the local LG Community Centers.

Other Marketing Strategies

Web sites are also an option but they require constant maintenance and upkeep. If you do not have the time or the inclination to review your Web site on a weekly basis, forgo this option, or hire a law student to update it for you.

An tried-and-true option is the Yellow Pages ad. Check your local Yellow Pages and see if lawyers are targeting the LG community. Not many are. Most people look to the Yellow Pages when looking for a lawyer. Maximize the ad you already run by adding a few words such as "Domestic Partner Agreements." You can also be more avant-garde and include "lesbian," "gay," or "same-sex."

A more subtle approach involves the use of graphics. A rainbow flag or pink triangle included in the ad will pull in LG clients. In fact, you need do nothing more. The rainbow and pink triangle are generally connected with the gay community.

You will be unique and the Yellow Pages can be a good source of advertising for a niche practice. You can include information on your practice that may not fit in a twenty-second radio commercial.

One additional source of referrals is the local bar association's lawyer referral service. Say that you offer services to the gay community. It is unlikely that many other attorneys earmark that niche in their listing.

Television advertising is expensive; however, you may be able to find some that is affordable. It will not be in prime time, but you may be able to find a late-night show that is popular with the LG community.

Commercial radio advertising is more affordable than television for the smaller marketing budget. Public radio can be another outlet for your marketing dollars. Sponsoring a particular show on public radio will get your name out to an audience considered more educated and older.

Teaching

Ever thought about teaching? There is a boon in law school courses that address issues affecting the lesbian and gay community. These courses also deal with bisexual and transgendered issues. Teaching such a class is another way to market your practice and establish yourself as an expert in the area. This can cause the media to turn to you when they need a comment. That, in turn, can bring clients to your doorstep.

LG concerns are not limited to a specific class. The issues range from family law to contracts to trusts and estates to taxes and constitutional law. You can offer to teach on an adjunct basis. You can also prepare a CLE course for the local bar association and present yourself as an attorney on the cutting edge of legal issues.

Conclusion

Marketing to a targeted audience requires creativity and innovation. Contact an advertising agency familiar with the LG community. They can assist you in directing your marketing efforts in the most cost-effective and efficient manner. The legal profession underserves the LG community. The laws affecting lesbians and gay men, and their families, are changing rapidly. With those changes will come more opportunities for talented lawyers to provide legal services to the LG community. Those changes will also mean confusion and contradiction between local, state, national, and foreign laws. Lesbians and gay men need lawyers who can clearly explain the changing legal landscape and how those changes affect them.

APPENDIX A

Estate Planning Forms

Form 1   Initial Estate Planning Appointment Letter
Form 2   Joint Representation Agreement
Form 3   Confidential Will Questionnaire
Form 4   Letter for Drafts of Documents
Form 5   Will Format
Form 6   General Durable Power of Attorney
Form 7   Language for Creating a Springing Durable Power
          of Attorney
Form 8   Designation of Agent
Form 9   Parental Consent to Authorize Medical Treatment of Minors
Form 10   Nomination of Guardian for Estate and Person of a Minor
          Child
Form 11   Authorization to Consent to Medical, Surgical, or Dental
          Examination or Treatment of a Minor and Authorization
          to Deal with Minor's School
Form 12   Priority of Visitation Language
Form 13   Client Estate Planning Checklist
Form 14   Notice of Revocation of Power of Attorney
Form 15   Domestic Partnership Agreement (Complex)
Form 16   Domestic Partnership Agreement, Separate Property (Simple)
Form 17   Domestic Partnership Agreement, Shared Property (Simple)
Form 18   Termination of Domestic Partnership
Form 19   Shared Parenting Agreement
Form 20   Nomination of Guardian for Adult
Form 21   Additional Clauses for Domestic Partnership Agreements
Form 22   Authorization to Release Health Information and/or
          Medical Records Protected Under the Health Information
          Portability and Accounting Act (HIPAA)

ESTATE PLANNING FORM 1

Initial Estate Planning Appointment Letter

Your Letterhead

Date

Client Name/Address

Dear_____:

In preparation for the initial interview I am enclosing a questionnaire. I ask that you each complete an individual questionnaire. The information will help in preparing your estate documents.

We will review the questionnaires at the time of the interview. You can mark down any additional questions, issues, or ideas you have. You can also call me with any questions.

We will also discuss health care powers of attorney, durable powers of attorney for finances, and designation of agent.

I know your privacy is important. I understand you trust me to protect the confidentiality and security of that information. The information I collect from you will be used only to provide the legal services you request. All of your information is held in strict confidence and is not released to anyone, except as agreed to by you, or as required under any applicable law. I am bound by professional standards of confidentiality that are more stringent than any required by law.

My representation of both of you together is desirable to develop a coordinated plan. However, representing both of you in the privileged attorney-client relationship is not without its possible, even if remote, disadvantages. Having separate lawyers would ensure that each of you has your own advocate providing independent advice. You would also be assured that all communications to your separate lawyers would remain privileged and confidential, even from each other.

As a couple in a committed relationship, you have a special and unique connection and generally share mutual goals and aspirations. Future circumstances could arise, however, in which your separate financial or legal interests might diverge. Depending on such future circumstances, it is possible that my joint representation of both of you together could require me to withdraw and recommend that you consult different lawyers in the future. This is in accordance with my professional ethics. I do not presently foresee such a situation, but it remains a possibility.

In a joint representation I cannot serve as an advocate for one of you against the other. I cannot negotiate on behalf of one with the other. Instead, I will assist both of you in jointly developing a coordinated, overall estate plan that is beneficial and acceptable to both of you. In order to develop such a plan it is necessary that each of you be completely candid in advising me of all relevant information that may affect your estate plan. As a consequence of my advising both of you jointly, any information I receive from either of you that may affect the estate plan of the other will not be confidential between the two of you. I am required to disclose this information to the other. In all other respects our communications are privileged and confidential.

I am attaching my fee schedule for your review.

I look forward to working with you in developing a successful estate plan. Call me if you have any questions.

Sincerely,

Your Attorney
Attorney at Law

ESTATE PLANNING FORM 2

Joint Representation Agreement

It is the policy of _____, Attorney at Law, to advise couples in committed relationships that each of you is entitled to be represented by your own attorney. By signing this agreement, you have authorized me to represent both of you in your estate planning.

I cannot be an advocate for one of you against the other if I represent both of you. Information either of you gives me relating to your will and your general estate plan cannot and will not be kept by me from the other. You have asked me to advise you jointly, so my effort will be to assist you in developing a coordinated overall estate plan. I will also encourage the resolution of any differences of opinion or conflicting interests in an equitable and logical manner. As to those matters on which your individual interests may differ, I will attempt to explain to both of you the interests of each of you and the effect a particular course of action will have on you individually.

By signing this letter, each of you confirms that you have requested and consented to me jointly representing both of you in connection with the preparation of your wills and your general estate plan. Each of you agree that communications and information I receive from either of you that is relevant to your wills and general estate plan will not be kept confidential from the other. You also understand that if a conflict of interest arises between the two of you I will be ethically obligated to withdraw from representing either of you. At that time I will encourage both of you to retain independent counsel.

ACCEPTED AND AGREED

Date: _____   _____

Date: _____   _____

ESTATE PLANNING FORM 3

Confidential Will Questionnaire

Please answer the following questions. Your answers provide a basis for discussing your specific estate plan needs and intentions. The answers will be used to draft your documents. Please answer the questions as completely as possible. If certain questions do not apply to you, please mark them as "N/A." All information supplied is strictly confidential and necessary to provide you with proper advice. We will discuss any questions you have about the requested information when we meet.

1. Your legal name: _____
2. Partner's legal name: _____
3. Do you currently have a will? [ ] Yes (Please have it available)   [ ] No
4. Home address: _____
   Telephone number: _____
5. Date of birth: _____
   Place of birth: _____
   Citizenship:_____
6. Have you been married? [ ] Yes   [ ] No
   If "Yes" did marriage end in [ ] death or [ ] divorce?
   Year marriage ended: _____
   If there was a divorce, please have a copy of the divorce decree available.
7. Do you have a domestic partnership agreement in effect? [ ] Yes   [ ] No
   If "Yes" please have a copy available for review.
8. Do you have any children? [ ] Yes   [ ] No
   (Skip to Question 9 if you have no children)
   a. Do any of your children have special needs or are any handicapped?
      [ ] Yes [ ] No
   b. Who has physical custody of the children? _____
   c. Please list all of your children, including adopted children. Include names, city, state, and ages.

Name	City, State	DOB
_____	_____	_____
_____	_____	_____
_____	_____	_____

   d. Please identify any children who may have predeceased you:
      _____
      _____

(Use other side if additional space is needed)

Specific Bequests of Property to Specific Persons

In many situations a person tells family members how (s)he wants the personal property divided. Generally, these items are not specifically mentioned in the will. This leaves you free to create a separate list that you may change whenever you like without having to rewrite your will. You can use the will to make a specific bequest if you are concerned your wishes will not be honored. A specific bequest may also be appropriate if you intend to leave an item to a nonfamily member.

9. Please indicate the specific item(s) you want distributed and the name of the person(s) to whom you are leaving the item(s). _____
    _____
    _____
    (Use other side if additional space is needed)

10. PETS. If you have pets you may want to consider what happens to them after your death. You may want to provide that a specific individual cares for your pets. In that situation, you may want to provide a specific monetary bequest to that person for the care of the pet. _____
    _____
    _____

Beneficiaries of Your Estate

Please think about who you want to name to inherit your estate. You must also consider who will inherit the balance of your property (after the executor distributes the specific bequests, if any). Example: Do you want everything to go to your partner? If you have children, do you want to provide for them? Grandchildren? Other family members? Do you want everyone to receive equal shares?

11. Name the person(s) to whom you want to leave your estate:
    Name: _____
    Relationship: _____
    City/State: _____
    Name: _____
    Relationship: _____
    City/State: _____
    (Use other side if additional space is needed)

12. Name the person(s) you wish to be the alternate beneficiary of your estate:
    Name: _____
    Relationship: _____
    City/State: _____
    Name: _____
    Relationship: _____
    City/State: _____
    Name: _____
    Relationship: _____
    City/State: _____
    (Use other side if additional space is needed)

13. GUARDIANSHIP OF MINOR CHILDREN. If you have children under the age of 18 you need to consider naming a guardian. Natural parents have priority in these matters. You can name someone to be the guardian of the person and of the estate. If you do not name a guardian, and there is no other natural parent, the probate court will appoint one for any minor child(ren).

    a. First choice for guardian:

    Name: _____
    Relationship: _____
    City/State: _____

    b. Alternate choice for guardian:

    Name: _____
    Relationship: _____
    City/State: _____

14. EXECUTOR. Every will needs an individual to act as the executor. This is the person responsible for collecting all the property at the time of death and paying all legal debts, taxes, and expenses out of the property collected. The executor is also responsible for distributing the remaining property to the people named in your will. The executor can be anyone over the age of eighteen or it can be an institution. It is advisable to name an alternate executor in case the first person is unable or unwilling to accept the responsibility. Your executor will be compensated from the estate assets according to a schedule set by [your state] law. The executor may choose to waive the fee.

    a. First choice for executor:

    Name: _____
    Relationship: _____
    City/State: _____

    b. Alternate choice for executor:

    Name: _____
    Relationship: _____
    City/State: _____

15. WILL CONTEST. Consider whether any family member is apt to file a will contest. If you think that may happen, you may want to include a provision to deter people from filing a will contest. You may provide that anyone contesting the will receives nothing from the estate. Generally, you will need to leave a specific bequest sufficient to make an heir think twice before contesting your will.

16. TAX ISSUES. In order to determine if tax planning is required for your estate it is important to estimate the overall value of your accumulated property. This includes life insurance and all property listed in your name. The 2004 exemption for federal estate tax is $1.5 million. If your total estate is over $1 million more extensive estate planning may be required. We will discuss the alternatives at the interview.

Estimated value of your total assets at present: (Check one)
a.   [ ] Under $1 million
b.   [ ] Over $1 million

17.   Do you want to sign a durable power of attorney for finances? [ ] Yes   [ ] No
     a.   Whom do you want to name as your attorney-in-fact (the person to whom you are giving the authority to act on your behalf)?

Name: _____

Address: _____

Telephone number: _____

Relationship: _____

     b.   Alternate Attorney-in-fact:

Name: _____

Address: _____

Telephone number: _____

Relationship: _____

18.   Do you want to sign a health care power of attorney and living will? [ ] Yes [ ] No
     a.   First choice (the person designated to make health care decisions for you):

Name: _____

Address: _____

Telephone number: _____

Relationship: _____

     b.   Alternate choice:

Name: _____

Address: _____

Telephone number: _____

Relationship: _____

19.   Do you want to execute a designation of agent? This document allows you to name someone to make decisions concerning who will visit you in a health care facility (including nursing home and hospice), disposition of personal effects, disposition of remains, and funeral arrangements. While these documents have not been tested in court, it does give you the opportunity to make your intentions known. [ ] Yes   [ ] No

Assets

Generally, a will does not list each and every item of property that you want to convey following your death. However, it is important to list the *form of ownership and the approximate value of your property.* If you are unsure as to the form of ownership you can ask your insurance agent or your mortgage holder. If you are still uncertain please have the documents available and we will review them together. It is important that you complete the answers concerning the following assets as best you can.

20. a. REAL PROPERTY (e.g., residence, vacant land, rental property, vacation home). Please have your deeds available for review.

(i) Location: _____

Market value and mortgage balance: _____

Exact way owner(s) are named on deed: _____

_____

(ii) Location: _____

Market value and mortgage balance: _____

Exact way owner(s) are named on deed: _____

_____

(Use other side if additional space is needed)

b. BANK ACCOUNTS (Indicate whether checking, savings, brokerage account, or CDs)

Name/location of financial institution:_____

Account balance: _____

Name of account holder (specify if joint or payable on death): _____

Name/location of financial institution: _____

Account balance: _____

Name of account holder (specify if joint or payable on death): _____

Name/location of financial institution: _____

Account balance: _____

Name of account holder (specify if joint or payable on death): _____

Name/location of financial institution:_____

Account balance: _____

Name of account holder (specify if joint or payable on death): _____

(Use other side if additional space is needed)

c. IRAs, RETIREMENT PLANS (including 401k accounts)

Name/location of financial institution: _____

Account balance: _____

Name of account holder: _____

Name of beneficiary: _____

Name/location of financial institution: _____

Account balance: _____

Name of account holder: _____

Name of beneficiary: _____

Name/location of financial institution: _____

Account balance: _____

Name of account holder: _____

Name of beneficiary: _____

Name/location of financial institution:_____

Account balance: _____

Name of account holder: _____

Name of beneficiary: _____

(Use other side if additional space is needed)

d.   STOCKS, BONDS, MUTUAL FUNDS, INCLUDING U.S. SAVINGS
     BONDS

Name(s) of stocks/bonds/funds: _____

How holdings are held: _____

Approximate value: _____

Name(s) of stocks/bonds/funds: _____

How holdings are held: _____

Approximate value: _____

Name(s) of stocks/bonds/funds: _____

How holdings are held: _____

Approximate value: _____

(Use other side if additional space is needed)

e.   TITLED VEHICLES; list all cars, trucks, boats, and motorcycles:

Year/make/model: _____

Titled owner: _____

Approximate value: _____

Year/make/model: _____

Titled owner: _____

Approximate value: _____

(Use other side if additional space is needed)

f.   OTHER IMPORTANT ASSETS (e.g., stamp/coin/other collections, busi-
     ness interests, partnerships, lottery winnings):

_____

_____

_____

(Use other side if additional space is needed)

g.   LIFE INSURANCE POLICIES

Name on policy: _____

Face value: _____

Beneficiary: _____

Name on policy: _____

Face value: _____

Beneficiary: _____

(Use other side if additional space is needed)

Please note any additional questions you want to discuss during the interview.

ESTATE PLANNING FORM 4

Letter for Drafts of Documents

Your Letterhead

Date

Client Names/Address

Dear _____:

I am enclosing the drafts of the following documents:

1. Wills
2. Durable Powers of Attorney for Finances
3. Designation of Agent
4. Health Care Powers of Attorney
5. Living Wills

Please review the documents. Let me know, either by phone or letter, if you need or want to make any changes. Once you review the documents, and any changes are made, we can arrange to sign everything.

I look forward to hearing from you.

Sincerely,

Your Attorney
Attorney at Law
Enc.

ESTATE PLANNING FORM 5

Will Format

Last Will and Testament

of

_____

I, _____, of _____, _____, hereby make, publish, and declare this to be my Last Will and Testament and revoke all previous wills and codicils made by me.

Section 1. Identification of Family
1.01   My partner's name is _____. All references in this will to my partner, whether or not specifically named, shall mean only my partner, _____.

1.02   I have (no) living children or issue. [Specify names of children and whether they are minors or adults. If minors, will must also include a Guardian of Person and Estate clause in conformance with state law. Include the partner's children in the definition of children whether biological or adopted; include any children where the partner's adoption petition has not been finalized.]

Section 2. Nomination of Executor
2.01   I hereby nominate _____ to serve as my Executor. Should this person be unable or unwilling at any time to serve as my Executor, I nominate _____ of _____, _____, to serve as my Alternate Executor.

2.02   I direct that my Executor, and any successor thereto, be permitted to serve without bond in any jurisdiction.

Section 3. Disposition of Tangible Personal Property
3.01   I give, devise, and bequeath my tangible personal property to my partner, _____. My Executor may, in his/her sole discretion, sell any of the property that, in his/her opinion, is not suitable for distribution, and the proceeds thereof shall become a part of my residuary estate. If the devisee named in this section does not survive me, I direct that the said property be disposed of or distributed with the residue of my estate.

Section 4. Residuary Devise
4.01   The balance of my residuary estate shall consist of all property or money owned by me at the time of my death and not otherwise effectively disposed of in this will, including all insurance proceeds or other death benefits that are payable to

my estate but excluding any property over which I may have a power of appointment, less all valid claims asserted against my estate and all expenses incurred in administering my estate, including expenses of administering nonprobate assets.

4.02 I give, devise, and bequeath the balance of my residuary estate to my partner, _____, if he/she survives me.

4.03 If my partner predeceases or fails to survive me I give, devise, and bequeath the balance of my residuary estate to _____.

4.04 I am leaving my estate to my partner, _____, because he/she is my life partner. I am not making these provisions out of any disrespect or lack of affection or love for my family. It is my intention that my partner, _____, inherit my estate. [Also, see proposed clause in Chapter 4.]

Section 5. Specific Provision Regarding My Pet(s)

5.01 If my partner, _____, predeceases or fails to survive me, I bequeath any pets I may own at the time of my death to _____. He/She is willing and able to maintain my pets in a comfortable setting with a standard of care similar to that which I had provided for them. I bequeath to _____, for accepting my pets under the foregoing sentence, the sum of $500 per pet. This bequest is made with the intention that such amount shall defray the costs of providing care to my pets, but without any restriction or obligation to account to any person for the use of such funds.

5.02 If _____ is unable to accept and care for my pets, I authorize and request my Executor to select an appropriate person who is willing and able to do so and to maintain my pets in a comfortable setting with a standard of care similar to that which I had provided for them. I bequeath to the person accepting my pets under the foregoing sentence the sum of $500 per pet. This bequest is made with the intention that such amount shall defray the costs of providing care to my pets, but without any restriction or obligation to account to any person for the use of such funds.

Section 6. Powers of Executor

6.01 My Executor, and any successor thereto, shall have all of the powers granted to Executors and fiduciaries under the probate code and other applicable laws of the state of _____, including the power to execute any joint or individual tax return on my behalf or on behalf of my estate.

6.02 My Executor shall be entitled to reasonable compensation for services actually performed and to reimbursement of expenses properly incurred.

a. My Executor shall have, in addition to any other powers, the power to invest, reinvest, sell, mortgage, lease, or otherwise transfer or dispose of any part or all of my estate, without the necessity of obtaining prior or subsequent court approval;

b. To make repairs or improvements to my property as may be deemed necessary to preserve or enhance the value of my estate;

c. To borrow funds for use in estate administration if there are insufficient liquid assets in my estate;

d. To employ persons, including attorneys, investment advisors, or other agents for assistance or advice, or not to employ such persons, as my Executor deems appropriate;

e. To compromise and settle any claims against or in favor of my estate on such terms and conditions as my Executor deems best;

f.   To make determinations as to the allocation of receipts and the apportionment of expenditures between income and principal. My Executor shall not be required to follow any provision of law regarding such determinations, including [relevant chapter of state code].

6.03   My Executor may make distributions either in cash or in kind. Distributions in kind may be made at the discretion of my Executor. My Executor may make any distributions under this will either (1) directly to the beneficiary, (2) in any form allowed by applicable state law for gifts or transfers to minors or persons under disability, (3) to the beneficiary's guardian, conservator, or caregiver for the benefit of the beneficiary, or (4) by direct payment of the beneficiary's expenses.

Section 7. Construction and Definitions

The following rules and definitions shall apply in the construction of this instrument and in the administration of my estate:

7.01   Any reference to my "Executor" in whatever form refers to the person, persons, or institution then acting as the personal representative of my estate.

7.02   If any devisee or other beneficiary under this will dies within 30 days after my death or under such circumstances where there is insufficient evidence in the judgment of my Executor to determine whether such person has died within 30 days after my death, the devisee or beneficiary shall be deemed to have failed to survive me.

7.03   The laws of the state of _____ shall govern all questions as to the validity and construction of this.

7.04   The term "estate and death taxes" shall mean all estate, inheritance, transfer, succession, or other taxes or duties payable by reason of my death, including interest and penalties thereon.

Section 8. Payment of Taxes and Expenses

8.01   I direct my Executor to pay the expenses of administering my estate, the expenses created by reason of my death, and all estate and death taxes payable with respect to property includable in my gross estate or taxable by reason of my death, whether or not such property is part of my probate estate and whether or not such taxes are payable by my estate or by the recipient of any such property. Such taxes and expenses should be paid out of my residuary estate without apportionment.

[Optional Clause]

8.02   I direct my Executor to pay only those expenses dealing with my funeral and interment that conform to my expressed wishes. If anyone interferes with my expressed wishes concerning my funeral, memorial service, or interment, and fails to abide by those expressed wishes, that person or persons shall be wholly responsible for any and all expenses. I ask that the Court and all concerned persons in this regard honor my expressed wishes, even if those wishes run counter to those of my immediate family.

IN WITNESS WHEREOF, I hereby subscribe my name to this instrument this _____ day of _____, 20__, at _____, _____.

_____
Testator

Statement of Witnesses

Each of the undersigned declares, under penalty of perjury and the laws of the State of _____, that the following is true and correct. I am over the age of eighteen years and competent to be a witness to the will of _____. He/She signed the foregoing instrument on the _____ day of _____, 20__, declaring it to be his/her Last Will and Testament in the presence of each of us. We, at the testator's request and in the testator's presence, and in the presence of each other, now subscribe our names as witnesses.

We do hereby declare that the testator signed and executed the instrument, as his/her last will, that he/she signed willingly and that he/she executed it as his/her free and voluntary act for the purposes therein expressed. We also declare that each of the witnesses, in the presence and hearing of the testator, signed the will as witness and that to the best of his or her knowledge the testator was at the time eighteen or more years of age, of sound mind, and under no constraint or undue influence.

_____

Witness Signature

_____

Witness Name

_____

Witness Address

_____

Witness Signature

_____

Witness Name

_____

Witness Address

ESTATE PLANNING FORM 6

General Durable Power of Attorney

Warning to Person Executing This Document

This is an important and powerful document. It creates a durable power of attorney. Before executing this document you should know these facts:

1. This document provides the person you designate as your attorney-in-fact with broad powers to dispose, sell, convey, and encumber your real and personal property.

2. These powers will exist for an indefinite period of time unless you limit their duration in this document. These powers will continue to exist even if you become disabled, incapacitated, or incompetent.

3. You have the right to revoke or terminate this durable power of attorney at any time; however, you must do so in writing.

I, ___(principal's name)___ of ___(principal's address)___, the Principal, hereby create this General Power of Attorney for the purpose of enabling the Agent named below to act as my agent and attorney-in-fact on all matters at all times, either before or after my disability.

1. **Designation of Agent.** I hereby designate and appoint ___(agent's name)___ of ___(agent's address)___ to be my agent and attorney-in-fact to act in my name and stead for all purposes.

In the event that my designated agent named above shall, at any time, be unable or unwilling to serve, or continue to serve, as my agent and attorney-in-fact, I hereby designate and appoint ___(alternative agent's name)___ of ___(alternative agent's address)___ to be my agent and attorney-in-fact to act in my name and stead for all purposes.

2. **Effective Date.** This General Power of Attorney and the powers conferred herein shall be effective as of the date I execute this document as set forth below.

3. **Disability or Disappearance of Principal.** This General Power of Attorney shall not be affected by my disability. The powers and authority conferred to my agent _____ in this instrument shall be fully exercisable by him/her notwithstanding my subsequent disability or incapacity or any later uncertainty as to whether I am alive or dead. All acts performed by my agent pursuant to this General Power of Attorney during any period of my disability or incompetence or during any period of uncertainty as to whether I am alive or dead shall have the same effect and inure to the benefit of and bind me, my heirs, devisees, and personal representative, to the same extent as if I were alive, competent, and not disabled.

4. **Nomination of Guardian of Person and Estate.** In the event I become disabled and am unable to manage my own affairs, I hereby nominate _____ as the Guardian of my person and estate. I nominate him/her as my Guardian

because he/she is best suited to carry out my wishes, desires, and intentions concerning my estate. He/She is also the person who has my best interests at heart. I trust him/her completely and ask the Probate Court to honor my selection of my Guardian. I also ask that my nominee serve without bond.

In the event the Probate Court does not name my nominee as the Guardian of my person and estate, I demand that the person selected by the Court be required to post a bond to serve in the capacity of Guardian.

5. **Powers of Agent.** The Agent acting under this General Power of Attorney shall have the full power and authority to do and perform every act and thing to the same extent as I could do if personally present and under no disability. The Agent shall have all of the powers, rights, discretions, elections, and authority conferred by statute, the common law, or rule of court or governmental agency that are reasonably necessary for the Agent to act on my behalf for any purpose. In addition to these general powers, the Agent shall have the following specific powers:

a. The power to request, ask, demand, sue for, recover, sell, collect, forgive, receive, and hold money, debts, dues, commercial paper, checks, drafts, accounts, deposits, legacies, bequests, devises, notes, interests, stocks, bonds, certificates of deposit, annuities, pension and retirement benefits, insurance proceeds, any and all documents of title, choses in action, personal and real property, intangible and tangible property and property rights, and demands whatsoever, liquidated or unliquidated, as now are, or may become, owned by, or due, owing, payable, or belonging to me, or in which I have or may hereafter acquire an interest; to have, use, and take all lawful means and equitable and legal remedies, procedures, and writs in my name for the collection and recovery thereof, and to adjust, sell, compromise, and agree for the same; and to make, execute, and deliver for me, on my behalf and in my name, all endorsements, acceptances, releases, receipts, or other sufficient discharges for the same.

b. The power to prepare, sign, and file joint or separate income tax returns or declarations or estimated tax returns for any year or years; to prepare, sign, and file gift tax returns with respect to gifts made by me, or by the Agent on my behalf, for any year or years; to consent to any gift and to utilize any gift-splitting provision or other tax election; and to prepare, sign, and file any claim for refund of any tax. This power is in addition to and not in limitation of the tax powers granted in the next paragraph.

c. The power and authority to do, take, and perform each and every act and thing that is required, proper, or necessary to be done, in connection with executing and filing any tax return, receiving and cashing any refund checks with respect to any tax filing, and dealing with the Internal Revenue Service and any state and local tax authority concerning any gift, estate, inheritance, income, or other tax, and any audit or investigation of same. This power shall include the power to do all acts that could be authorized by a properly executed Form 2848, entitled "Power of Attorney and Declaration of Representative," granting the broadest powers provided therein to the Agent.

d. The power to conduct, engage in, and transact any lawful matter of any nature, on my behalf or in my name, and to maintain, improve, invest, manage, insure, lease, or encumber, and in any manner deal with any real, personal, tangible, or intangible property, or any interest in them, that I now own or may later acquire, in my name and for my benefit, upon such terms and conditions as the Agent shall deem proper.

e.   The power to exercise or perform any act, power, duty, right, or obligation that I now have, or may later acquire, including, without limiting the foregoing, the right to enter into a contract of sale and to sell any real, personal, tangible, or intangible property on my behalf and the right to renounce or disclaim any testamentary or nontestamentary transfer intended for me.

f.   The power to make, receive, sign, endorse, acknowledge, deliver, and possess insurance policies, documents of title, bonds, debentures, checks, drafts, stocks, proxies, and warrants, relating to accounts or deposits in, or certificates of deposit, other debts and obligations, and such other instruments in writing of any kind or nature as may be necessary or proper in the exercise of the rights and powers herein granted.

g.   The power to sell any and all shares of stocks, bonds, or other securities now belonging to or later acquired by me that may be issued by any association, trust, or corporation, whether private or public, and to make, execute, and deliver any assignment or assignments of any such shares of stocks, bonds, or other securities.

h.   The power to conduct or participate in any business of any nature for me and in my name; execute partnership agreements and amendments thereto; incorporate, reorganize, merge, consolidate, recapitalize, sell, liquidate, or dissolve any business; elect or employ officers, directors, and agents; carry out the provisions of any agreement for the sale of any business interest or the stock therein; and exercise voting rights with respect to stock, either in person or by proxy, and exercise stock options.

i.   The power to enter any safe deposit box rented by me, and to remove all or any part of the contents thereof, and to surrender or relinquish said safe-deposit box. Any institution in which any such safe-deposit box may be located shall not incur any liability to me or my estate as a result of permitting the Agent to exercise the powers herein granted.

j.   The power to make outright gifts of cash or property to adults or to minors in custodial form under an applicable Gifts to Minors Act, in amounts not to exceed Eleven Thousand Dollars ($11,000.00) to each adult or minor donee in any calendar year. Permissible donees hereunder shall include my partner, any of my children or stepchildren and their descendants, or any descendant of a brother or sister of mine or of any person to whom I shall have been married, as well as any person who shall be married to any of the foregoing.

k.   To make gifts to facilitate my qualifying for the receipt of government benefits for my long-term health care and nursing home care needs (e.g., old age pension and Medicaid benefits). Any gifts made pursuant to this paragraph are to be made unconditionally as determined in the sole discretion of my attorney-in-fact. Such gifts shall be irrevocable. My attorney-in-fact is authorized to make said gifts so long as my long-term care is reasonably provided for by my assets subject to this Power, or otherwise during the time period I would be disqualified from receiving long-term care and/or medical assistance under the State Medicaid program. Any gifts may be made outright or in trust and may include both real and personal property.

l.   The power to convey or assign any cash or other property of which I shall be possessed to the trustee or trustees of any trust that I may have created, provided that such trust is subject to revocation by me, which power shall be exercisable hereunder by the Agent.

m. The power to purchase United States Government Bonds known as "Flower Bonds," which may be used in payment of death taxes from my estate.

n. Subject to the provisions of Section 1 above, the power to appoint a substitute or alternate agent and attorney-in-fact, who shall have all powers and authority of the Agent.

6. **Limitation of Power of Agent.** Notwithstanding any other provision of this General Power of Attorney, the Agent shall have no rights or powers hereunder with respect to any act, power, duty, right, or obligation relating to any person, matter, transaction, or property held or possessed by me as a trustee, custodian, personal representative, or other fiduciary capacity. In addition, the Agent shall have no power or right to perform any of the following functions:

7. **Ratification.** I hereby ratify, acknowledge, and declare valid all acts performed by the Agent on my behalf prior to the effective date of this General Power of Attorney.

8. **Revocation and Termination.** This General Power of Attorney is revocable by me, provided that insofar as any governmental agency, bank, depository, trust company, insurance company, other corporation, transfer agent, investment banking company, or other person who shall rely upon this power, this power may be revoked only by a notice in writing executed by me and delivered to such person or institution.

This General Power of Attorney shall not be revoked or otherwise become ineffective in any way by the mere passage of time, but rather shall remain in full force and effect until revoked by me in writing.

I hereby revoke any and all general powers of attorney previously executed by me, if any, and the same shall be of no further force or effect. However, I do not intend in this General Power of Attorney to affect, modify, or terminate any special, restricted, or limited power or powers of attorney previously granted by me in connection with any banking, borrowing, or commercial transaction.

9. **Construction.** This General Power of Attorney is executed and delivered in the State of _____, and the laws of the State of _____ shall govern all questions as to its validity and as to the construction of its provisions. This instrument is to be construed and interpreted as a general durable power of attorney. The enumeration of specific powers is not intended to limit or restrict the general powers granted to the Agent in this instrument.

10. **Reliance.** Third parties may rely upon the representations of the Agent as to all matters related to any power granted to the Agent in this instrument, and no person who acts in reliance upon the representation of the Agent shall incur any liability to me or my estate as a result of permitting the Agent to exercise any power. Third parties may rely upon a photocopy of this executed General Power of Attorney to the same extent as if the copy were an original of this instrument. This document consists of [number of] pages of which this is the last.

IN WITNESS WHEREOF, I have executed this Durable Power of Attorney on the _____ day of _____, 20___.

_____
Principal

State of _____
County of _____

_____, the Principal, personally appeared
before me and executed and acknowledged this Durable Power of Attorney for
Finances before me this _____ day of _____, 20_____.

_____
Notary Public

ESTATE PLANNING FORM 7

Language for Creating a Springing Durable Power of Attorney

"This power of attorney shall be effective only after any one licensed physician shall have signed and caused to be attached to this power of attorney his or her written statement indicating that I am incapable in his or her judgment of attending effectively to my financial affairs by reason of mental or physical disability."

"This written statement shall be acknowledged before a Notary Public. All persons relying on any such written statements attached to this power of attorney may presume that the identity and qualifications of the person signing any such statement are what they purport to be. There shall be no duty to make further inquiry or investigation beyond the review of each written statement itself. No physician furnishing any such written statement shall be liable to me or any other person for furnishing the same in good faith, for the disclosure of any information about me or my financial affairs contained in the statement, nor for any act or omission of my attorney-in-fact."

ESTATE PLANNING FORM 8

Designation of Agent

I, _____, designate my partner, _____,
to be my agent empowered with the following authority.

1. VISITATION AUTHORITY: To give notice that, if I am admitted to a medical
facility of any type, a nursing home, hospice, or similar health care, skilled nursing, or
custodial facility, my agent, _____, shall be designated as
"family" as that term is defined by the Joint Commission on Accreditation of Healthcare Organizations. JCAHO defines "family" as "The person(s) who plays a significant role in the individual's [patient's] life. This may include a person(s) not legally
related to the individual." (Joint Commission Resources, JCR, *2001 Hospital Accreditation Standards,* p. 322).

My agent shall have priority in being admitted to visit me in such facility. My
partner, as my agent, is designated as the person to be consulted by medical or
health care personnel concerning my care and treatment. This is in keeping with the
Health Care Power of Attorney I executed. My agent shall also have the authority
to determine who will be permitted to visit me while in the facility and during any
recovery at home.

This authorization supersedes any preference given to parties related to me by
blood or by law or other parties desiring to visit me. These instructions shall remain
in full force and effect unless and until I freely give contrary written instructions to
competent medical personnel on the premises involved. My subsequent disability or
incapacity shall not affect these instructions.

2. RECEIPT OF PERSONAL PROPERTY: My agent shall also have the right
to receive any and all items of personal property and effects that may be recovered
from or about my person by any hospital, nursing home, other health care facility,
police agency, or any other person or public/private entity at the time of my illness,
disability, or death. This specifically includes cash or other liquid asset(s).

**3. DISPOSITION OF REMAINS/AUTOPSY AUTHORIZATION/FUNERAL
ARRANGEMENTS:** My agent shall have the authority to authorize an autopsy if
it is deemed necessary or is required by law. In matters concerning the disposition
of my remains and funeral arrangements, I provide that my agent/partner, or any
other person directed to dispose my remains, shall follow my instructions for any
funeral services. Any limitations on this authority are specified in this document.

My agent is to direct the disposition of my remains by the following method:
burial _____ cremation _____. The specific instructions are found in

_____
_____.

In this regard, my agent has the authority to make all decisions necessary for my
obituary notice, funeral, any mortician's role therein, burial services, interment or
cremation of my body, including, but not limited to the selection of a casket or urn,

selection, care and tending of a grave site, and selection of a gravestone including the inscription thereon.

4. SPECIFIC INSTRUCTIONS CONCERNING MY AGENT'S AUTHORITY OR LIMITATIONS THEREON: My agent shall have access to all medical records and information pertaining to me and concerning treatments, procedures, treatment plans, etc. This includes the right to disclose this information to other people. I explicitly authorize any medical or health care provider to release information requested by my agent to him/her and consider my agent an authorized person to receive such information under the Health Information Portability and Accessibility Act (HIPAA).

My agent has the authority to admit or discharge me from any hospital, nursing home, residential care, assisted living or similar facility, or service entity. My agent also has the authority to hire and fire medical, social service, and other support personnel. My agent is primarily responsible for my medical and health care.

_____   _____
Date   Principal

State of _____
County of _____

Before me, a Notary Public in and for said County and State, personally appeared the above named, _____, who acknowledged that he/she did sign the foregoing two-page instrument, and that the same is his/her free act and deed.

In Testimony Whereof, I have hereunto set my hand and official seal at _____, _____, this _____ day of _____, 20___.

_____
Notary Public

ESTATE PLANNING FORM 9

Parental Consent to Authorize Medical Treatment of Minors

I/We, _____, am/are the parent(s) of _____, born [date of birth for each minor child]_____. I am/We are placing my/our child(ren) into the care of _____ during our absence. I/We authorize _____ to consent to any medically necessary X-ray, examination, anesthetic, medical or surgical diagnosis or treatment, and hospital care recommended for the benefit of my/our child(ren). Such medical care is to be rendered to said child under the care, supervision, and advice of a physician or other medical care provider licensed to practice medicine in any state in the United States. I/We further authorize _____, to consent to any X-ray, examination, dental or surgical diagnosis or treatment, and hospital care to be rendered to my/our minor child(ren) by a dentist licensed to practice dentistry in any state in the United States.

    This authority shall be valid from _____ to _____, 20___.

    Executed this _____ day of _____, 20___ at _____, _____.

_____
Parent's Signature

_____
Parent's Signature

State of _____
County of _____

On _____, 20___, _____

_____, personally appeared before me and executed this document. WITNESS my hand and official seal.

_____
Notary Public

ESTATE PLANNING FORM 10

Contributed by Susan M. Murray, Attorney at Law
Langrock Sperry & Wool, LLP
111 S. Pleasant St.
P. O. Box 351
Middlebury, VT 05753-0351
(802) 388-6356; smurray@langrock.com

Nomination of Guardian for Estate and Person of a Minor Child

I, _____, the natural mother/father of the minor child, _____, who was born on _____, hereby make the following nomination of a legal guardian of the person and property of my minor child, in the event I am unable, physically or mentally, to care for my child.

I

In the event I become unable to care for my minor child, it is my desire, and I hereby nominate, my friend, companion, and life partner, _____, currently residing in _____, _____, to be the legal guardian of the person and property of my minor child, _____. He/She is to serve without having to post a bond.

This nomination is based on the fact that a loving and parental relationship exists between _____ and _____. Furthermore, my minor child, _____, has lived with this adult and looks to him/her for guidance, support, and affection. It would be detrimental to my child, _____, to deprive him/her of this established relationship at a time when I am unable to provide the security and care necessary to my child's health development. It is in the child's best interest that _____ be named the guardian of my minor child.

It is my strong belief that it would be in _____'s best interests to be placed in the care and custody of _____ notwithstanding the interest or availability of each and every one of my family members so to act as guardian.

I have chosen _____ as _____'s guardian because he/she is the person most suitable and capable of helping and guiding _____. I believe that _____ can and will provide a warm, stable, and loving home for my child, and care for him/her and teach him/her with understanding and love.

I have given this matter long and careful contemplation before choosing any guardian for my child. I have considered each of my family members as well as close friends as possible guardians. After long and thoughtful reflection, for all of the above reasons, I firmly believe that it will be in _____'s best interests that _____ be named guardian of the person and estate (property) of my minor child in the event of my disability.

II

In the event that _____ is unable to serve as guardian or is disqualified by a Court of law from serving, I nominate _____ to serve as the guardian of the person and property of my child, _____.

III

[Both the identity and whereabouts of the minor child's natural father are unknown to me.]

or

[The minor child was conceived through alternative insemination by an anonymous donor and has no natural father.]

or

[The minor child was conceived through alternative insemination by donor. Said donor waived, in writing, any and all rights he may have to object to my nomination of a guardian.]

I have purposefully not nominated my parents or siblings to be the guardians of my child in the event of my disability. It is my belief that they lack an established, close, and warm relationship with my child. I believe it would be detrimental to _____ to remove him/her from _____ and place him/her with adults who are, for all practical purposes, strangers.

IN WITNESS WHEREOF, I have hereunto signed my name this _____ day of _____, 20___.

_____
Client's Name

Witnesses

_____ executed this document, consisting of _____ pages in our presence. At his/her request, and in his/her presence, we have hereunto subscribed our names as attesting witness thereto. Each of us declares that _____ appears to be of sound mind and free from duress or undue influence at the time he/she signed this document. He/She affirmed that he/she is aware of the nature of the document and signed it freely and voluntarily.

_____ Residing at _____
_____ Residing at _____

State of _____
County of _____

At _____, _____ on the _____ day of 20__, _____ personally appeared before me. He/She acknowledged this instrument, by him/her sealed and subscribed, to be his/her free act and deed.

_____
Notary Public

ESTATE PLANNING FORM 11

Contributed by Susan M. Murray, Attorney at Law
Langrock Sperry & Wool, LLP
111 S. Pleasant St.
P. O. Box 351
Middlebury, VT 05753-0351
(802) 388-6356; smurray@langrock.com

Authorization to Consent to Medical, Surgical, or Dental Examination or Treatment of a Minor and Authorization to Deal with Minor's School

I, _____, being the mother of _____, a minor child, do hereby authorize _____ of _____, _____, to consent to any X-ray examination, anesthetic, medical or surgical diagnosis or treatment and hospital care to be rendered to said minor child under the general and/or special supervision and upon the advice of a physician and/or surgeon licensed to practice medicine in any state of the United States, or to consent to any X-ray, examination, anesthetic, dental or surgical diagnosis or treatment, and hospital care to be rendered to said minor child by a dentist licensed to practice dentistry in any state of the United States.

I direct any hospital, medical staff, or physician treating said minor child to give to _____ the same priority in visitations that would be extended to me as said minor child's mother in the event that said minor child is a patient in any hospital or other health care facility.

I authorize any school, day care, or similar institution providing services to me for my minor child, _____, to release any and all records, information, or documentation relating to said minor child to _____.

I further direct such school, day care, or institution to accept _____'s signature or consent in lieu of mine with regard to parental authorization to enable said minor child to take part in outside or in-school activities or day care activities, to sign for report cards or similar notices, to provide notice of said minor child's absence from school, and the like.

I further authorize these acts as the sole physical and legal custodian of said minor child under the laws of the State of _____.

In the event of emergency, I direct that the school, day care, or institution make a reasonable effort to contact _____ and me immediately.

I further direct that in a medical emergency the school, day care, or other institution has my permission to send said minor child immediately to a hospital with a trauma center that is reasonably close to the place where such medical emergency took place.

I declare that any act lawfully done or authorized hereunder by _____ shall be binding on myself, my heirs, legal and personal representatives, and assigns. I agree for myself, my heirs, and assigns to hold same harmless and indemnify all persons, hospitals, agencies, and/or institutions acting in reasonable reliance on the authority herein conferred.

IN WITNESS WHEREOF, I have hereunto signed my name this _____ day of _____, 20__ at _____, _____.

_____
CLIENT'S NAME

State of _____
County of _____

At _____, _____, on the _____ day of 20__, _____ personally appeared before me. He/She acknowledged this instrument, by him/her sealed and subscribed, to be his/her free act and deed.

_____
Notary Public

ESTATE PLANNING FORM 12

Contributed by Matthew R. Dubois, Attorney at Law
Vogel & Dubois
550 Forest Ave., Ste. 205
Portland, ME 04104
(207) 761-7796; info@maine-elderlaw.com

Priority of Visitation Language

[Can be used in a health care power of attorney, a living will, or a designation of agent form.]

In the event of my incapacity, my Agent, _____, shall be afforded the first opportunity to visit with my attending physician and me.

If I am unable to express my own desires regarding visitation or discuss my care with my attending physician, my Agent shall have the sole right to decide when and if other parties may visit with my attending physician or me. My Agent shall have the authority to limit subsequent contact by third parties and relatives with my attending physician and myself.

This provision is intended to clearly establish my Agent's authority over my blood relatives or legal representatives who may hold priority over visitation, health care decisions, and conference with treating physicians, in the event of my incapacity, under applicable law or custom.

ESTATE PLANNING FORM 13

Client Estate Planning Checklist

This list is designed to assist you or your heirs in locating important documents and information needed to settle your estate. You should review this document regularly and update as needed.

1. Will
   a. Date signed: _____
   b. Where located: _____
   c. Name of executor: _____
2. Trust
   a. Date signed: _____
   b. Where located: _____
   c. Name of trustee: _____
3. Durable power of attorney for finances
   a. Date signed: _____
   b. Where located: _____
   c. Name of attorney-in-fact: _____
4. Living will
   a. Date signed: _____
   b. Where located: _____
5. Health care power of attorney
   a. Date signed: _____
   b. Where located: _____
   c. Name of attorney-in-fact: _____
6. Health insurance
   a. Name of carrier: _____
   b. Carrier's address/phone number: _____
   c. Policy number: _____
7. Disability insurance
   a. Name of carrier: _____
   b. Carrier's address/phone number: _____
   c. Policy number: _____
8. Long-term care insurance
   a. Name of carrier: _____
   b. Carrier's address/phone number: _____
   c. Policy number: _____
9. Life insurance
   a. Name of carrier: _____
   b. Carrier's address/phone number: _____
   c. Policy number: _____
   d. Named beneficiary: _____

10. Retirement/employee benefits
    a. Company name, address, and phone number: _____
    b. Named beneficiary: _____
11. Letter of instructions (funeral and burial; insurance papers; location of will and trust; location of safe deposit box; names/addresses/phone numbers of lawyer, accountant, broker, and clergy member; instructions for distribution of tangible personal property; expression of wishes for family/friends; business instruction)
12. Personal financial information including credit cards, loans, checking and savings accounts, brokerage accounts, stocks, bonds and U.S. savings bonds, mutual funds, outstanding loans both owing and owed
13. List of doctors
14. Statement of wishes concerning personal matters
15. Current and complete references to all personal property currently owned
16. Location of business buy/sell agreements, partnership papers, corporate filings, and other business-related paperwork
17. Irrevocable insurance trust
18. Specification of all property, individual, joint, community, and mixed
19. Any gift tax returns filed? When/Where/Type of gift
20. Deeds to all real property

ESTATE PLANNING FORM 14

Notice of Revocation of Power of Attorney

I, _____, of _____, City of
_____, County of _____, State
of _____, hereby give notice that I have revoked, and do
hereby revoke, the power of attorney dated _____, given to
_____ [name of attorney-in-fact], empowering said
_____ to act as my true and lawful attorney-in-fact,
and I declare that all power and authority granted under said power of attorney is
hereby revoked and withdrawn.

DATED: _____   _____

WITNESSES: Signature of Principal

_____ Residing at _____
_____ Residing at _____

State of _____
County of _____

    On this _____ day of _____, 20__, _____ person-
ally appeared before me and executed this document in my presence.

_____

Notary Public

Estate Planning Form 15

Contributed by Lisa Ayn Padilla, Attorney at Law
Gibbons, Del Deo, Dolan, Griffinger & Vecchione, P.C.
One Pennsylvania Plaza, 37th Floor
New York, NY 10119-3701
(212) 554-9621 (voice)
(973) 639-6228 (fax)
LPadilla@gibbonslaw.com
www.gibbonslaw.com

Domestic Partnership Agreement (Complex)

AGREEMENT, made this _____ day of _____, 20__, between _____,
residing at _____ [hereinafter referred to as "_____"],
and _____, residing at _____ [hereinafter referred
to as "_____"].

WHEREAS, the parties intend to establish a domestic partnership and raise
children together, and desire to set forth their agreements and expectations regarding their financial, property, and other rights and obligations arising out of the contemplated domestic partnership; and,

WHEREAS, by execution of this Agreement, the parties hereby revoke and nullify any and all written agreements previously executed by either or both parties; this Domestic Partnership Agreement supersedes any and all previously executed or unexecuted Domestic Partnership Agreements between the parties;

NOW, THEREFORE, in consideration of the mutual promises and agreements herein contained, the parties hereto agree as follows:

1. Separate Property of Each Party

The parties wish to identify what will remain the separate property of each party during the domestic partnership, and to determine their rights in the event of a separation or dissolution of their domestic partnership, as hereinafter discussed.

The following shall constitute and remain the "separate property" of the respective parties: (a) property, whether real or personal, and whether vested, contingent, or inchoate, belonging to or acquired by a party prior to the contemplated domestic partnership of the parties, including without limitation the property listed on Schedules A-1 and A-2; (b) all property acquired by a party at any time by bequest, devise, inheritance, distribution from a trust, or by gift; (c) salary, wages, and other compensation for personal services; (d) retirement and pension benefits; (e) compensation for personal injuries; (f) proceeds of insurance policies received from any sources; (g) the increase in value of such property, whether or not such increase in value is due in whole or in part to the contributions or efforts of the other party; (h) rents, issues, profits, dividends, interest, or other income derived from other distributions upon such property; (i) the proceeds of the sale of such property; (j) property acquired in exchange for such property or acquired with the proceeds of the sale of such property; (k) any other property identified or defined as separate property elsewhere in this Agreement; and (l) any assets or property acquired at any time by either party in their singular name or jointly with another person. It is the agreement of the parties that unless property is denoted in this Agreement as joint property, it shall be considered separate property. Except as otherwise expressly provided in this Agreement, or by way of an addendum to this Agreement, each party shall be responsible for his/her own debts, unless a debt was undertaken in a joint manner, as evidenced by the documents creating such debt. Each party hereby indemnifies and holds harmless the other for any debt incurred by the party that is not a joint debt.

Except as otherwise expressly provided in this Agreement, each party shall keep and retain sole ownership, enjoyment, control, and power of disposal of his/her separate property of every kind and nature, now owned or hereafter acquired by such party, free and clear of any interest, rights, or claims of the other party by reason of the domestic partnership or otherwise. These rights include the right to dispose of his/her separate property by gift, sale, testamentary transfer, or in any other manner, and to encumber, pledge, or hypothecate such property.

Each party covenants and agrees not to make any claim or demand on the separate property of the other party or on the heirs, legal representatives, executors, or administrators of the other party with respect to the separate property of the other party, except as otherwise may be expressly provided in this Agreement.

If the parties commingled their separate property to acquire new property, the interests of the parties in this new property shall be separate property interests in proportion to their original contributions to the acquisition of such property.

Except as otherwise expressly provided in this Agreement, the separate property now or hereafter owned by one party can become joint or the property of the other party only by a written instrument reclassifying the property for purposes of this Agreement executed by the party whose separate property is thereby reclassified. No acts, conduct, or statements by either party shall change the status of separate property, other than an instrument executed by the party whose separate property is thereby reclassified.

No contribution by either party to the care, maintenance, improvement, custody, or repair of the separate property of the other party, whether such contributions are in the form of money, property, or personal services rendered, shall in any way alter or convert any of such separate property, or any increase in the value thereof, to the status of joint property. Any contributions by either party to the care, maintenance, improvement, custody, or repair of the separate property of the other party shall become part of the separate property of the other party, and the contributing party shall not have any claim for reimbursement. No use by either party of earnings or other separate property for joint or household expenses shall be construed to imply joint ownership of such assets.

Each party agrees, upon request, to cooperate with the other in connection with procuring loans secured by the other party's separate property, including the execution of instruments waiving all rights with respect to the other's separate property. The party owning the separate property shall indemnify and hold the party requested to execute such instruments harmless from and against any liability with respect thereto. Any proceeds derived from loans secured by a party's separate property shall be said party's separate property.

2. Joint Property

The parties recognize that they may from time to time acquire property in their joint names. This may include, for example, sums deposited into bank accounts in their joint names and stock and bond portfolios, certificates of deposit, and money market funds in their joint names.

Title to any and all savings accounts, certificates of deposit, money market certificates, cash reserve accounts, money management accounts, stocks, bonds, savings plans, securities, or any other funds or assets of the same or a similar nature (other than joint checking accounts) acquired jointly by both of the parties during the domestic partnership shall be placed in the names of both parties hereto in such manner that such assets may not be withdrawn or disposed of without the signatures of both parties thereto.

3. Gifts

All gifts given to the parties jointly shall be the joint property of the parties. Any gifts given from one party to the other prior to or during the domestic partnership shall be considered the separate property of the recipient of the gift, unless the party making the gift specifies that the property is to be the joint property of the parties. Such specification shall be in writing and attached to this Domestic Partnership Agreement as an Attachment.

4. General Living Expenses

The day-to-day living expenses of the parties, such as normal expenses for food, clothing, and entertainment, shall be paid by the parties in such proportions as they from time to time may agree upon in light of the then available resources of each party.

5. Joint Checking Account

The parties shall establish a joint checking account from which either party may withdraw funds for the payment of household and other joint living expenses, including living expenses of the child(ren). The parties shall contribute funds to this checking account as they from time to time may agree in light of the available resources and income of each party.

The funds in this checking account, and property purchased using these funds, shall be the joint property of the parties. This checking account is for the convenience of the parties, and the amounts deposited in the account are not intended to reflect the actual cost of living of either or both of the parties.

6. The Parties' Residence

_____ and _____ are the owners of a house known as _____ (primary residence).

Said primary residence is encumbered by a mortgage and the principal balance presently outstanding is approximately $_____.

It is the intention of the parties to reside in said primary residence with their children.

The expenses of ownership of the primary residence, including without limitation utilities, homeowners insurance, real estate taxes, maintenance, and ordinary repairs, shall be paid by the parties in such proportions as they from time to time may agree upon in light of the then available resources of each party.

If, during the domestic partnership, the primary residence is sold and another residence is purchased in its place, the substitute residence shall be treated in the same manner under this Agreement as the primary residence for which it was substituted, unless the parties otherwise agree in a written instrument amending this Agreement.

The furniture, furnishings, and other household effects in the primary residence shall be the joint property of the parties, with the exception of items that were the pre-domestic partnership separate property of either party and art, antiques, or collectibles acquired as separate property of either party.

7. Other Real Estate

The parties from time to time may own real property other than the primary residence. If a party acquires such property in his/her sole name, it shall be said party's separate property for purposes of this Agreement. If the parties acquire such property as tenants in common, the interests of each party shall be separate property interests in the proportions set forth in the deed. If the parties acquire such property as joint tenants with rights of survivorship, it shall be joint property. The rights of the parties with respect to such property shall be governed by this Agreement unless they agree to some other treatment of such property in a written instrument amending this Agreement.

8. Pensions

Any pension plans of either party, heretofore or hereafter created, shall be and shall remain separate property of such party, free from any claim of the other party, notwithstanding the domestic partnership of the parties. Any pension plans that are the separate property of a party shall not be subject to equitable distribution and shall not be considered assets to which the other party would be entitled to share in, unless, in the event of death, the other party is designated on the pension plan documents as a beneficiary.

As used herein, "pension plan" shall mean any kind of pension plan, 401(k) plan, retirement plan, profit sharing plan, employee benefit plan, or any other form of deferred compensation to which a party may be entitled because of his/her employment or work. References to a party's pension plan shall be deemed to include all monies held in such party's pension plan or thereafter added to or accumulated in that pension plan, and any increments, accretions, or increases in the value of such pension plan, and any other rights such party has to the pension plan or such monies.

9. Children

It is the intention of the parties to have or adopt one or more children during the domestic partnership. It is the intention of the parties that during their domestic partnership, when one partner has a child, that partner will consent to the other partner's undertaking of any and all steps to adopt that child.

It is the intention of each party to create an irrevocable life insurance trust that will be funded by their separate funds, and that will provide for the maintenance of the surviving partner, if the domestic partnership is still in effect at the time the other partner dies. Regardless of the status of the domestic partnership, the irrevocable life insurance trust will provide for the maintenance, health, education, and welfare of the parties' child(ren). The parties agree that each will continue to fund their own irrevocable life insurance trust until such time the life insurance policy has been paid in full or the youngest child reaches the age of twenty-five. The parties hereby agree that all indicia of life insurance shall be set forth in Schedule C, attached hereto.

10. Termination of the Domestic Partnership

The parties recognize that it is in their best interests to set forth their agreement as to their respective rights in the event of a termination of their domestic partnership by separation or dissolution of their domestic partnership.

The parties agree that the value of the primary residence and/or any other property that is owned jointly or by another entity whereby both are beneficiaries or own an equitable interest shall be determined by obtaining a current appraisal from the lending institution that possesses a mortgage on the property. If either party feels the lending institution's appraisal is inaccurate, then a second appraisal will be obtained at the cost of the party seeking another appraisal. Both appraisals will be averaged and that average shall be the price the parties will use to determine the fair market value of the property.

The parties intend to agree upon which party will be able to remain in the primary residence, depending upon a variety of factors, the most important factor being the best interest of their child(ren). To exercise the option to purchase the primary residence one party (the Proposed Buyer) must give the other party (the Proposed Seller) written notice of her election to purchase the Proposed Seller's interest within 90 days after termination of the domestic partnership. Termination of the domestic partnership shall be considered as written notice defined herein. If the parties cannot agree upon which party will remain in the primary residence, the primary residence will be placed with a real estate broker at listing price of the fair market value as determined by the method set forth above.

If practicable, the closing of title shall take place on a date not more than 60 days after the fair market value of the primary residence is determined. At the closing of title, the Proposed Buyer shall pay the amount due to the Proposed Seller and the Proposed Seller shall deliver good and clear title, free from encumbrances, and any documents that may be necessary or appropriate to transfer all of his/her right, title, and interest in the primary residence to the Proposed Buyer.

If either party elects to purchase the interest of the other party in the primary residence, the party who so elects shall also simultaneously purchase the interest of the other party in the jointly owned furniture, furnishings, and other household effects of the residence for the fair market value of such interest.

If neither party exercises the aforesaid options, the primary residence shall be promptly listed for sale with a broker mutually agreeable to the parties. The parties shall jointly agree to the listing price. If the parties cannot agree, then the average of the appraisals discussed earlier in this section shall be used to determine the listing price.

If the primary residence does not sell at the listing price within a reasonable period of time, said price shall be reduced until the residence is sold. A reasonable period of time is agreed upon to be six to eight months. The parties agree that the reduction in price will begin at five percent of the listing price. The reduction will continue in increments of five percent until the primary residence is sold.

The net proceeds from the sale of the primary residence, after deducting for all related expenses in connection with the sale, shall be divided equally between the parties. Any liens and encumbrances levied against the primary residence as the result of a debt owed by either party shall be paid by that party with his/her own separate assets prior to the passing of title to the Proposed Buyer.

In the event of the termination of the domestic partnership, the parties shall have joint legal custody of any minor children of the parties. It is the expectation of the parties that the children will reside predominantly with their respective birth or legal parent[; however, the other party shall have frequent and meaningful contact/ parenting time with the child(ren)].

Each party agrees to pay reasonable amounts, in light of his/her available income and resources, for the support of any minor children of the parties, at a minimum, in an amount that is set forth in the current child support guidelines of the state in which the parties reside. The parties agree to consult and negotiate in good faith regarding the children's education, visitation, payment of medical expenses, and other issues that may arise regarding the children in the event of the termination of the domestic partnership.

In the event of the termination of the domestic partnership any joint property acquired by the parties during the domestic partnership shall be divided equally between the parties, notwithstanding the percentage contribution each party may have made to acquire or create such property.

The parties recognize that some items of joint property, such as tangible personal property, cannot be readily divided into shares. If the parties cannot agree on the division of any such items or the fair compensation that one party should pay to the other for his/her share of such items, such items shall be sold so that the proceeds of sale may be divided equally.

Each party hereby irrevocably waives, releases, and relinquishes any and all claims or rights that he/she now or hereafter might otherwise have to or against the separate property now owned or hereafter acquired by the other party. This includes, without limitation, laws relating to equitable distribution, marital property, community property, curtesy, dower, or any other interest or right of distribution of property by reason of domestic partnership, cohabitation, union, or marriage. Each party recognizes that this waiver includes rights he/she might otherwise have or acquire in the future under the laws of the state in which the parties resided at the time the domestic partnership terminated.

As used herein, the term "termination of the domestic partnership" shall mean either party sending the other party written notice of intent to terminate the domestic partnership.

Notice shall be sent by first class mail, certified mail, or any other form of mailing by which confirmation of delivery can be ascertained. Notice shall be sent to the party's current residence where that person normally receives mail or to the party's last known address.

11. Death of the Parties

The parties recognize that it is in their best interests to set forth their Agreement as to their respective rights upon the death of either party during the domestic partnership.

All jointly owned property shall pass in accordance with the laws of the state in which the property is located. Title to property held jointly with rights of survivorship will pass to the survivor in accordance with state law.

Each party retains sole control over his/her separate property. Each party shall have the right to dispose of that separate property either by will or inter vivos or in accordance with the rules of intestate succession of the state in which the decedent was domiciled.

Nothing in this Agreement shall restrict the right of either party to bequeath or give property to the other party. If either party should provide that the other party shall receive property, as a bequest or gift under his/her last will and testament or otherwise, including without limitation life insurance proceeds, pension or profit sharing plan benefits, and assets held as joint tenants with rights of survivorship, such other party shall have the right to receive such property. The parties agree, however, that no promises of any kind have been made by either of them to the other with respect to any such bequest or gift.

The obligations set forth in this Article 11 shall terminate and cease to be binding in the event of the termination of the domestic partnership by separation or dissolution of their domestic partnership or annulment, except separate property shall always remain separate property.

If, upon the death of either party, an action for separation or dissolution of their domestic partnership or annulment has been commenced but a judgment has not been entered, any rights of the surviving party to share in the estate of the deceased party shall be extinguished and the surviving party shall be entitled to receive from the decedent's estate only what the surviving party would have been entitled to pursuant to the Agreement had a judgment of separation or dissolution of their domestic partnership been entered.

12. Full Disclosure

A copy of the parties' current net worth statement is attached hereto as Schedule B. The parties affirm that the contents of the net worth statement are accurate and true.

Each party has made independent inquiry, to his/her own satisfaction, into the complete financial circumstances of the other, and acknowledges that he/she is fully informed of the income, assets, and financial prospects of the other.

[Neither of the parties has been previously married. Neither of the parties has living children.]

13. Legal Representation

The parties acknowledge that they have retained and have been represented by separate and independent legal counsel of their own choosing in connection with the negotiation of this Agreement. _____ consulted with Attorney _____. _____ consulted with Attorney _____. Each has been separately and independently advised regarding this Agreement including the rights waived or otherwise released herein.

14. Notices

Any notice, demand, or other communication required or permitted under this Agreement shall be in writing and shall be delivered by hand or by courier or by certified or registered mail, return receipt requested, to a party at his/her address stipulated above or at such other address as the party may designate.

15. General Provisions

This Agreement is entire and complete and embodies all understandings and agreements between the parties. All prior understandings, agreements, conversations, communications, representations, correspondence, and other writings are merged into this instrument, which alone sets forth the understanding and agreement of the parties.

Each party acknowledges that all of the matters embodied in this Agreement, including all terms, covenants, conditions, waivers, releases, and other provisions contained herein, are fully understood by each; that this Agreement is fair, just, and reasonable; that each party is entering into this Agreement freely, voluntarily, and after due consideration of the consequences of doing so; and that this Agreement is valid and binding upon each party.

This Agreement and each provision thereof shall not be amended, modified, discharged, waived, or terminated except by a writing executed by the party sought to be bound. Failure of a party to insist upon strict performance of any provision of this Agreement shall not be construed as a waiver of any subsequent default of the same or similar nature, nor shall it affect the parties' rights to require strict performance of any other portion of this Agreement. Any waiver by either party of any provision of this Agreement or of any right or option hereunder shall not be deemed a continuing waiver and shall not prevent such party from thereafter insisting upon the strict performance or enforcement of such provision, right, or option.

The parties agree that each of them, upon request of the other party or the legal representatives of the other party, shall execute and deliver such other and further instruments as may be necessary or appropriate to effectuate the purposes and intent of this Agreement. Each party, upon request of the other, shall execute and deliver a confirmation that this Agreement remains in full force and effect.

This Agreement and all rights and obligations of the parties hereunder shall be governed by and construed in accordance with the laws of the State of _____. The laws of the State in which the parties reside with their child(ren) shall govern irrespective of whether either or both of the parties heretofore or hereafter reside or are domiciled in any other jurisdiction and irrespective of whether any property is located in any other jurisdiction. If any provision of this Agreement should be held to be invalid or unenforceable under the laws of any State, county, or other jurisdiction in which enforcement is sought, the remainder of this Agreement shall continue in full force and effect.

This Agreement shall be binding upon and shall inure to the benefit of the parties hereto and their respective heirs, executors, administrators, successors, and assigns.

IN WITNESS WHEREOF, the parties hereto have executed this Agreement on the date first written above, of their own free will, and attest that neither is under the influence of any alcohol, drug, or other substance that would affect the party's decision-making capability. Each party attests that he/she is competent to enter into this Agreement.

_____
Signature

_____
Signature

State of _____
County of _____

_____, the Principal, personally appeared before me and executed and acknowledged this Domestic Partnership Agreement before me this _____ day of _____, 20___.

_____
Notary Public

State of _____
County of _____

_____, the Principal, personally appeared before me and executed and acknowledged this Domestic Partnership Agreement before me this _____ day of _____, 20___.

_____
Notary Public

ESTATE PLANNING FORM 16

Domestic Partnership Agreement, Separate Property (Simple)

We, _____ and _____, make the following agreement:

   1.   We enter into this contract to set forth our rights and responsibilities to
each other. [Recite the consideration for the contract.]

   2.   We intend to abide by the provisions of this agreement in the spirit of love,
joy, cooperation, and good faith.

   3.   We agree that all property owned by either of us, as of the date of this
agreement, shall be considered to be and shall remain the separate property of each.
Neither of us will have any claim to the separate property of the other absent a written agreement transferring ownership. Lists of our major items of separate property
are attached and incorporated into this agreement.

   4.   Our individual income and any property accumulated from that income
shall remain the separate property of the person earning the income. Neither of us
shall have any claim to this separate property.

   5.   Each of us shall maintain separate bank accounts. This includes checking,
savings, and credit card accounts.

   6.   Neither of us shall be liable or responsible for the individual debts incurred
by the other in her/his own name.

   7.   We agree to be jointly responsible for all debts we enter into together.

   8.   We agree to equally divide all household and living expenses. This includes,
but is not limited to, groceries, utilities, rent, and daily household expenses.

   9.   We agree that there may be a need to maintain a joint bank account
(checking or savings) for a specific purpose. In that event, we agree to contribute an
equal amount to the bank account. Neither party will have the right to withdraw
funds from that account without the permission and consent of the other.

   10.   We also agree that we may, at some time, agree to own property jointly.
Any jointly held property ownership shall be reflected either in writing or on the
title to said property. In the event we dissolve our domestic partnership, we provide
that any jointly held property will be divided into equal shares, unless we provide
otherwise in a written document.

   11.   Any property received by one of us through gift or inheritance remains the
separate property of the recipient. The other party has no claim on that separate
property unless provided for in a written instrument.

   12.   Neither of us has any rights to, nor any financial interest in, any real estate
owned entirely or partially by the other person. This includes any real property
accumulated before or during our relationship.

   13.   We agree that either party can terminate this contract by giving the other
party a one-week written notice of that intent. If either of us seriously considers

leaving the relationship we both agree to at least three counseling sessions with a professional counselor or therapist.

14.   In the event that this relationship is terminated we agree to divide all jointly held property equally. Neither of us shall have any claim against the other for support, property, or financial assistance.

15.   We agree to resolve any dispute arising from this agreement through mediation. The mediator shall be an objective third party who is mutually agreed upon. The mediator's role shall be to help us dissolve our relationship and resolve any differences concerning a division of jointly held property or other issues in a mature and unemotional manner. We agree to enter into mediation in good faith.

16.   In the event that our attempt at good-faith mediation is unsuccessful to resolve all issues in dispute, either party may seek to resolve the issues through arbitration through the use of the following protocol:

    a.   Deliver a written demand for arbitration to the other person and name one arbitrator;

    b.   The other party shall respond with the name of a second arbitrator within five days from receipt of the notice;

    c.   The two named arbitrators shall select and name a third arbitrator;

    d.   The arbitration meeting will take place within seven days following the selection of the third arbitrator;

    e.   Each party is entitled to retain legal counsel at his/her own expense;

    f.   Each party may present witnesses and evidence at the arbitration hearing;

    g.   The arbitrators shall issue their decision within five days after the hearing. Their decision shall set forth their findings and conclusion and shall be in writing. The decision shall be binding upon each of us. We agree that neither party shall seek relief from the arbitration decision in court.

    h.   If the person to whom an arbitration demand is made fails to respond within five days, the other party may give an additional five days' written notice of his/her intent to proceed. If there is still no response, the person initiating the arbitration may proceed with the arbitration before an arbitrator he/she has designated. Any award shall have the same force and effect as if all three arbitrators had settled it.

17.   This agreement represents our complete understanding concerning our domestic partnership. It replaces any and all prior agreements, written or oral. We agree that this document can be amended in only writing and must be signed by both of us.

18.   We agree that in the event a court finds any portion of this contract to be illegal or otherwise unenforceable, the remainder of the contract shall remain in full force and effect.

Signed this _____ day of _____, 20__, at _____,
_____.

_____   _____
Signature   Signature

State of _____

County of _____

_____ and _____ personally appeared before me and executed and acknowledged this Domestic Partnership Agreement before me this ____ day of _____, 20__.

_____

Notary Public

Exhibit A: Separate Property of _____

Exhibit B: Separate Property of _____

ESTATE PLANNING FORM 17

Domestic Partner Agreement, Shared Property (Simple)

We, _____ and _____, make the following agreement:

1. We enter into this contract to set forth our rights and responsibilities to each other.

2. We intend to abide by the provisions of this agreement in the spirit of love, joy, cooperation, and good faith. [Specify the consideration for the contract].

3. We agree that all property owned by either of us, as of the date of this agreement, shall be considered to be and shall remain the separate property of each. Neither of us will have any claim to the separate property of the other absent a written agreement transferring ownership. A list of our major items of separate property are attached and incorporated into this agreement.

4. Our individual income, earned while we are living together and during this relationship, shall belong to both of us in equal shares. Likewise, all property accumulated from that income shall belong to both of us in equal shares. In the event we separate and/or terminate this domestic partnership we agree to divide all such accumulated property, in whatever form, equally between us.

5. We agree to maintain joint bank accounts. This includes checking and savings accounts. In the event we decide to obtain a joint credit card account we agree to be jointly liable for the credit card balance.

6. Neither party shall be responsible or liable for any credit card debt incurred by the other on his/her individual credit card accounts.

7. Neither of us shall be liable or responsible for the debts incurred by the other as an individual.

8. We agree to be jointly responsible for all joint debts and expenses.

9. We agree to equally divide all household and living expenses. This includes, but is not limited to, groceries, utilities, rent, and daily household expenses.

10. We also agree that we may, at some time, agree to own real property jointly. Any jointly held real property ownership shall be reflected either in writing or on the title to said property. In the event we dissolve our domestic partnership, we provide that any jointly held property will be divided into equal shares, unless we provide otherwise in a written document.

11. Any property received by one of us through gift or inheritance remains the separate property of the recipient. The other party has no claim on that separate property unless provided for in a written instrument.

12. Neither of us has any rights to, nor any financial interest in, any separate real estate owned entirely or partially by the other person. This includes any real property accumulated before or during our relationship.

13. We agree that either party can terminate this contract by giving the other party a one-week written notice of that intent. If either of us seriously considers leaving the relationship we both agree to at least three counseling sessions with a professional counselor or therapist.

14. In the event that this relationship is terminated we agree to divide all jointly held property equally. Neither of us shall have any claim against the other for support, property, or financial assistance.

15. We agree to resolve any dispute arising from this agreement through mediation. The mediator shall be an objective third party who is mutually agreed upon. The mediator's role shall be to help us dissolve our relationship and resolve any differences concerning a division of jointly held property or other issues in a mature and unemotional manner. We agree to enter into mediation in good faith.

16. In the event that our attempt at good-faith mediation is unsuccessful to resolve all issues in dispute, either party may seek to resolve the issues through arbitration through the use of the following protocol:

    a. Deliver a written demand for arbitration to the other person and name one arbitrator;

    b. The other party shall respond with the name of a second arbitrator within five days from receipt of the notice;

    c. The two named arbitrators shall select and name a third arbitrator;

    d. The arbitration meeting will take place within seven days following the selection of the third arbitrator;

    e. Each party is entitled to retain legal counsel at his/her own expense;

    f. Each party may present witnesses and evidence at the arbitration hearing;

    g. The arbitrators shall issue their decision within five days after the hearing. Their decision shall set forth their findings and conclusion and shall be in writing. The decision shall be binding upon each of us. We agree that neither party shall seek relief from the arbitration decision in court.

    h. If the person to whom an arbitration demand is made fails to respond within five days, the other party may give an additional five days' written notice of his/her intent to proceed. If there is still no response, the person initiating the arbitration may proceed with the arbitration before an arbitrator he/she has designated. Any award shall have the same force and effect as if all three arbitrators had settled it.

17. This agreement represents our complete understanding concerning our domestic partnership. It replaces any and all prior agreements, written or oral. We agree that this document can be amended only in writing and must be signed by both of us.

18. We acknowledge that both of us have had the opportunity to consult with an attorney of our choice to review this document. We also acknowledge that each of us, as individuals, is responsible for consulting with an attorney. The failure or refusal of either or both of us to do so shall not be construed to mean this Domestic Partnership Agreement was not entered into willingly, freely, and voluntarily by both of us.

19. We agree that in the event a court finds any portion of this contract to be illegal or otherwise unenforceable, the remainder of the contract shall remain in full force and effect.

Signed this _____ day of _____, 20__, at _____,
_____.

_____   _____
Signature   Signature

State of _____
County of _____

_____ and _____, personally
appeared before me and executed and acknowledged this Domestic Partnership
Agreement before me this _____ day of _____, 20__.

_____
Notary Public

Exhibit A: Separate Property of _____
Exhibit B: Separate Property of _____
Exhibit C: Jointly Held Property of _____ and _____

ESTATE PLANNING FORM 18

Termination of Domestic Partnership

1.   It is hereby agreed that _____ and _____, who have been domestic partners living together at [specify address and type of premises, apartment or house], shall separate and go their own ways. At this time neither party has the intention of resuming their former domestic partnership arrangement.

2.   It is also agreed that each party shall retain complete and total control over his/her separate property, including any furnishings or furniture, that each brought into the relationship. A list of each party's separate property is attached hereto as Exhibit A.

3.   It is further agreed that the items listed in Exhibit B were purchased and are owned jointly by the parties. The parties divided these items in a fair and equitable manner. Each party is entitled to complete and total control over the items listed under their respective names in Exhibit B.

4.   The parties agree to dispose of any and all joint debts and other joint obligations in the following manner: [specify each creditor, amount owed, who will pay obligation, indemnification clause].

5.   The parties also agree [that both of them are leaving the shared premises] or [that _____ is leaving the shared premises and _____ will remain in the shared premises]. The one staying shall assume all responsibility for said premises from this date forward, except for any common debts incurred by the parties during their relationship. _____ will take whatever action is required to [remove _____'s name from the lease] or [refinance the mortgage].

6.   The party who is leaving agrees not to reenter the premises without the remaining party's permission, nor will he/she remove any items from the premises without the other party's knowledge.

7.   [Specify how jointly owned real estate is to be valued, listed, and sold].

8.   Neither party shall have any claim against the other party's business interests, pension or retirement funds, insurance proceeds, rights of inheritance, or any other property not specifically described in this Agreement.

9.   Neither party shall have a claim to compensation from the other for services rendered during the time they lived together, for financial support of any kind, or for any other property, assets, or money not described in this Agreement.

10.   The parties agree to resolve any dispute arising from this agreement through mediation. The mediator shall be an objective third party who is mutually agreed upon. The mediator's role shall be to help the parties dissolve their relationship and resolve any differences concerning a division of jointly held property or other issues in a mature and unemotional manner. The parties agree to enter into mediation in good faith. [Parties agree to engage attorneys practicing collaborative law in order to resolve the issues involved in the termination of their relationship.

Both parties understand that the collaborative process is engaged in with the specific intent to avoid litigation.]

11.   In the event that the parties' attempt at good-faith mediation is unsuccessful to resolve all issues in dispute, either party may seek to resolve the issues through arbitration through the use of the following protocol:

a.   Deliver a written demand for arbitration to the other person and name one arbitrator;

b.   The other party shall respond with the name of a second arbitrator within five days from receipt of the notice;

c.   The two named arbitrators shall select and name a third arbitrator;

d.   The arbitration meeting will take place within seven days following the selection of the third arbitrator;

e.   Each party is entitled to retain legal counsel at his/her own expense;

f.   Each party may present witnesses and evidence at the arbitration hearing;

g.   The arbitrators shall issue their decision within five days after the hearing. Their decision shall set forth their findings and conclusion and shall be in writing. The decision shall be binding upon each party. The parties agree that neither one shall seek relief from the arbitration decision in court.

h.   If the person to whom an arbitration demand is made fails to respond within five days, the other party may give an additional five days' written notice of his/her intent to proceed. If there is still no response, the person initiating the arbitration may proceed with the arbitration before an arbitrator he/she has designated. Any award shall have the same force and effect as if all three arbitrators had settled it.

12.   Each party states that he/she entered into this Agreement freely and voluntarily, without fraud, duress, threats, or coercion.

The parties, by signing below, indicate their intention to participate in this Agreement and the provisions set forth herein. Signed this ___ day of _____, 20__.

_____   _____
    Signature   Signature

State of _____
County of _____

_____ and _____, the Principals, personally appeared before me and executed and acknowledged this Termination of Domestic Partnership/Living Together Arrangement before me this ____ day of _____, 20__.

_____
Notary Public

ESTATE PLANNING FORM 19

Shared Parenting Agreement

This agreement is made this ＿＿ day of ＿＿＿＿＿＿＿＿, 20＿, by and between ＿＿＿＿＿＿＿＿＿＿＿＿＿＿＿＿＿ and ＿＿＿＿＿＿＿＿＿＿＿＿＿＿＿＿＿.

    In consideration of the promises made to each other, and in consideration of our mutual contributions toward the [creation by in vitro fertilization; artificial insemination] or [adoption] of a child [born] or [adopted] on the ＿＿ day of ＿＿＿＿＿＿＿, 20＿, and in acknowledgement that state law is unsettled in this area of parental rights, and in acknowledgement of the parties' mutual belief that the best interests of our child, ＿＿＿＿＿＿＿＿＿＿＿＿＿＿＿, require stable sources of financial, academic, medical, and emotional support, the parties enter into this Agreement to guarantee that their child will receive the full benefit of having each and both of the parties as parents, including current and future financial and emotional support and rights to inheritance, and to guarantee that both ＿＿＿＿＿＿＿＿＿＿＿＿＿＿ and ＿＿＿＿＿＿＿＿＿＿＿＿＿＿ shall be considered natural and legal parents of ＿＿＿＿＿＿＿＿＿＿＿＿＿.

    Therefore, we agree as follows:

    1.   Each party acknowledges and agrees that they live together in a primary family relationship and have since ＿＿＿＿＿＿＿＿＿＿＿＿＿＿. The parties further acknowledge that during the course of their relationship [＿＿＿＿＿＿＿＿＿＿＿＿＿＿ gave birth to ＿＿＿＿＿＿＿＿＿＿ (child or children) on ＿＿＿＿＿＿＿＿＿＿] or [they adopted ＿＿＿＿＿＿＿＿＿ (child or children) on ＿＿＿＿＿＿＿＿＿＿.]

    2.   The decision to have a child was a joint decision of the parties and was based on the commitment of each party to parent the child(ren) jointly. The parties acknowledge that both partners have been primary parents and caregivers to the child(ren) since birth.

    3.   Each party acknowledges and agrees that, while they now live together as a family, there may come a time when the parties no longer do so. In that event, the parties agree that they will continue to provide for their child(ren) as follows:

    a.   Both parties will have joint custody of the child(ren).

    b.   Both parties will take whatever action is necessary to obtain a shared parenting agreement from the court having jurisdiction over these matters.

    c.   The child will spend approximately one-half of his/her time with each parent. Each parent shall share equally in the responsibility for the care of the child(ren) during school vacations or illness either by personally caring for the child(ren) or making arrangements for proper care.

    d.   Each parent will pay one-half of the normal daily living expenses and costs of the child(ren) while they live together; or the entire cost of daily living expenses when the child(ren) is/are with each one, should they stop living together.

    e. Each parent shall claim the child(ren) as a dependent for tax purposes in alternate years. _____ shall claim the child(ren) during even numbered tax years and _____ during odd numbered tax years.

    f. Each parent shall maintain the child(ren) as a beneficiary(ies) of a life insurance policy in the minimum amount of _____ until the child(ren) shall attain the age of [majority] or [specify age].

    4. Both parents acknowledge and agree that all major decisions regarding the physical location, support, education, medical care, and religious training of the child(ren) shall be made by them jointly.

    5. Both parents agree that each will make a good faith effort to remain in _____ (name community) until the child(ren) complete high school. Neither parent may move out of the designated community without the prior written consent of the other parent. The other parent shall not unreasonably withhold such consent.

    6. The parties agree that should a significant discrepancy occur in their respective net monthly income, following a separation, they will negotiate child support payments consistent with the child support schedule then in effect in their State of domicile.

    7. Each parent agrees that, in the event either of them is no longer able to care and provide for the child(ren) because of death or legal disability, it will be in the best interests of the child(ren) to remain with the other parent. Neither parent will allow the child(ren) to be adopted by any other person so long as both parents are living.

    8. Each parent agrees that any dispute pertaining to this Agreement will be resolved through mediation. The mediator shall be an objective third party who is mutually agreed upon. The mediator's role shall be to help us resolve any disputes, dissolve our relationship, and/or resolve any differences concerning the child(ren). The parties agree to enter mediation in good faith. [Can include clause/provision concerning collaborative law efforts to resolve disputes in addition to, in lieu of, or as an alternative to mediation.]

    9. In the event that the parties' attempt at good-faith mediation is unsuccessful to resolve all issues in dispute, either party may seek to resolve the issues through arbitration through the use of the following protocol:

    a Deliver a written demand for arbitration to the other person and name one arbitrator;

    b. The other party shall respond with the name of a second arbitrator within five days from receipt of the notice;

    c. The two named arbitrators shall select and name a third arbitrator;

    d. The arbitration meeting will take place within seven days following the selection of the third arbitrator;

    e. Each party is entitled to retain legal counsel at his/her own expense;

    f. Each party may present witnesses and evidence at the arbitration hearing;

    g. The arbitrators shall issue their decision within five days after the hearing. Their decision shall set forth their findings and conclusion and shall be in writing. The decision shall be binding upon each of us. We agree that neither party shall seek relief from the arbitration decision in court.

h. If the person to whom an arbitration demand is made fails to respond within five days, the other party may give an additional five days' written notice of his/her intent to proceed. If there is still no response, the person initiating the arbitration may proceed with the arbitration before an arbitrator he/she has designated. Any award shall have the same force and effect as if all three arbitrators had settled it.

10. Each party understands that there are legal questions raised by the issues involved in this Agreement that are not yet settled by statute or prior court decisions. Notwithstanding the knowledge that certain clauses stated in this Agreement may be unenforceable in a court of law, the parties choose to enter into this Agreement to clarify their intent to jointly provide and nurture their child(ren), even when they are no longer living together in a single family residence.

11. Specifically, the parties recognize that the current state of law regarding financial support of children may not obligate the non-legally recognized parent to provide support to the child(ren).

12. The parties also recognize that current law gives the natural/legal parent no enforceable right to collect support on behalf of the child(ren) from the other parent.

13. Notwithstanding the current state of the law regarding support, each party agrees to support the minor child(ren) and to be bound by current and future support obligations for the child(ren) pursuant to the laws of the State in which the child is domiciled.

14. The parties intend that this Agreement create an enforceable right for either party to collect child support on behalf of the child(ren), including the right to request that support be extended beyond minority consistent with the child support laws of the State of domicile.

15. The parties agree to do everything legally possible to create a legal relationship between the child(ren) and the non-legally recognized parent, _____. This will be done for purposes of custody, visitation, support, inheritance, health care insurance, and guardianship of the minor child(ren).

16. Each party agrees to leave at least one-half of his/her estate to the child(ren). If a trust is created for the child(ren), the trustor shall name the other parent as the trustee. Likewise, both parties agree to name the other as the child(ren)'s guardian in their respective wills. The parties agree to jointly decide on an alternate guardian of the child(ren).

17. The parties intend this Agreement to guide the Court should one become involved in determining the best interests of the child(ren). The parties agree that the Court shall have jurisdiction over any disputes arising during the child(ren)'s minority regarding custody, support, or visitation.

18. The parties agree to participate in Court-ordered mediation concerning issues of custody or visitation and to be bound by court orders regarding the child(ren). Specifically, _____ agrees to be bound by a court order compelling him/her to pay support for the child(ren) or to have contact with the child(ren) on a set schedule. Likewise, _____, the natural parent, agrees to be bound by any court order granting visitation and/or joint custody to _____. Both parties agree that they will not raise legal arguments intended to interfere with the ongoing relationship between the other parent and the child(ren).

19.   The parties agree to put aside any personal differences they may have with each other, in the event of their separation or termination of the relationship, in order to do what is in the best interests of the child(ren).

20.   If either party contests the Court's jurisdiction over any dispute involving the child(ren), including custody, support, care, or visitation, then that party may be stopped from defeating the Court's jurisdiction by reason of having accepted the benefits of the mutual promises contained in this Agreement. It either party contests the Court's jurisdiction over any issue involving the custody, care, support, or visitation of the child(ren), and is successful in defeating the Court's jurisdiction, then that party shall be liable for liquidated damages in the amount of $_____ for each year that this Agreement was in effect. The contesting party shall also be responsible for paying all costs and attorney fees incurred by the defending party.

21.   This Agreement contains the entire understanding of the parties. There are no promises, understandings, agreements, or representations between them that are not reflected in this Agreement.

22.   Each party agrees that he/she signed this Agreement voluntarily and freely, of his/her own volition, without any duress of any kind whatsoever.

23.   Both parties acknowledge that legal counsel represented them in the discussions and negotiations that led to the creation of this Agreement. _____, Attorney at Law, represented _____. And, _____, Attorney at Law, represented _____. Each party acknowledges that he/she had legal advice prior to signing this Agreement and that each fully understands the terms of this Agreement.

IN WITNESS WHEREOF, the parties hereunto have executed this Agreement, on the ____ day of _____, 20__, in _____, _____.

Dated: _____   _____
                                        Signature

Dated: _____   _____
                                        Signature

State of _____
County of _____

_____ and _____ personally appeared before me and executed and acknowledged this Shared Parenting Agreement before me this ____ day of _____, 20__.

_____
Notary Public

ESTATE PLANNING FORM 20

Contributed by Susan M. Murray, Attorney at Law
Langrock Sperry & Wool, LLP
111 S. Pleasant Street
P. O. Box 351
Middlebury, VT 05753-0351
(800) 639-6356 (voice)
(802) 388-6149 (fax)
smurray@langrock.com

Nomination of Guardian for Adult

I, _____, of _____,
_____, in the County of _____ and the
State of _____, being of sound mind and body and being presently
able to manage, without the supervision of a guardian, all aspects of my personal
care and financial affairs, do hereby state, declare, and nominate as follows:

If there should ever come a time when I am found by a court of competent jurisdiction to be unable to manage, without the supervision of a guardian, some or all
aspects of my personal care or financial affairs, then it is my strong wish and desire
that my friend, companion, and life partner, _____,
be appointed my guardian, notwithstanding the willingness, capability, or availability of any of my near relatives so to serve.

It is my belief that _____ is the person most able
and likely to promote my well-being, protect me from violations of my human and
civil rights, and ensure that I receive those benefits and services that I may need to
develop and maximize my opportunity for self-reliance and social and financial
independence. It is my belief that _____ has the ability to carry
out all of the powers and duties of guardianship, and I trust _____'s
integrity and judgment in all matters relating to my personal care and financial
affairs.

IN WITNESS WHEREOF, I have hereunto signed my name this _____ day of
_____, 20__, at _____, _____.

_____

CLIENT'S NAME

Witnesses

_____ executed this document in our presence and each of us declares that _____ appears to be of sound mind and free from duress at the time he/she signed this document. _____ affirmed that he/she is aware of the nature of the document and is signing it freely and voluntarily.

_____ Residing at _____
_____ Residing at _____

State of _____
County of _____

At _____, _____, on the ____ day of 20__, _____ personally appeared before me. He/She acknowledged this instrument, by him/her sealed and subscribed, to be his/her free act and deed.

_____
Notary Public

Additional Clauses for Domestic Partnership Agreements

1. Consideration

The parties agree that they enter into this Domestic Partnership Agreement for good and valid consideration. That consideration is their mutual covenants and promises as expressed in this document.

2. Entire Agreement

The parties agree that this document [instrument, recitation] contains the complete and entire agreement [understanding] between them. Any and all prior representations, correspondence, communications, and the like are incorporated into this agreement either explicitly or implicitly. The provisions of this document constitutes the entire understanding of the parties as to their respective rights, duties, and obligations of their Domestic Partnership.

3. Hold Harmless and Indemnification Clause

In the event that either party defaults on or fails to abide by the terms of this Agreement, that party shall indemnify the other and hold him/her harmless for all reasonable costs and expenses, including but not limited to attorney fees, incurred in enforcing this Agreement. This indemnification includes any costs incurred by the nondefaulting party in asserting or defending any rights hereunder against the defaulting party or any third parties who may be cooperating with or encouraging the defaulting party.

4. Severability

In the event that a court of competent jurisdiction deems any clause or provision of this Agreement to be unenforceable or invalid, that clause or provision shall be severed from the agreement. All remaining clauses and provisions shall continue in full force and effect and shall be enforceable by the parties.

5. Absence of Duress or Intimidation

The parties acknowledge that they enter into this Agreement freely and without any intent to deceive. By their signatures they state that they are not entering into this Agreement as the result of undue influence, fraud, or distress (economic, physical, or emotional) of any kind. They state that they are competent to enter into this Agreement and do so willingly. They also state that no other person or persons have exerted any pressure or undue influence over them to sign this Agreement.

6. Statement of Intent of the Parties

The parties intend to treat their domestic partnership as if it were a marriage sanctioned by the laws of the State of _____. If the parties decide, at some future date, to terminate their domestic partnership they agree to resolve any disputes without resorting to litigation.

The parties agree it is their intent to use mediation, collaborative law, or binding arbitration to resolve their disputes. They agree to submit all issues they cannot resolve between themselves to binding arbitration. The arbitrator shall apply the property, debt, and maintenance laws of the State of _____ in resolving the issues presented by the parties.

The parties agree that the arbitrator shall be selected from a list provided by the American Arbitration Association. The parties also agree to submit to binding arbitration under the rules of the American Arbitration Association. The parties agree that each shall be responsible for one-half of the fees and costs associated with any binding arbitration.

The parties agree that for the purposes of this Agreement, their Domestic Partnership began on _____.

ESTATE PLANNING FORM 22

Authorization to Release Health Information and/or Medical Records Protected under the Health Information Portability and Accountability Act (HIPAA)

I, _____, am the patient and I authorize the disclosure and use of the designated health information as listed on this form. I authorize the custodian of this health information to permit the person or persons named in this form to review or inspect the health information. I also authorize the custodian of the HIPAA-protected health information to provide copies of the information to the named person or persons if requested to do so.

DOB: _____ Patient's Social Security No.: _____

Provide a specific and explicit description of the information to be released, including the date and place of service if applicable:

_____
_____
_____
_____
_____
_____

I authorize the following health care provider or custodian of records to release and disclose the described health information:

_____

I authorize the health care provider or records custodian to release and disclose the health information to my designee:

_____

This request is for the following purpose(s):
___ Personal injury litigation ___ Other pending litigation ____ Medical malpractice litigation ___ Other (describe): _____

My designee ___ is ___ is not authorized to disclose the described health information to others.

I have the right to revoke this Authorization, in writing, at any time by notifying the person named as my designee to request the information. I shall also notify any health care provider or records custodian named on this form. Any revocation shall be prospective in nature and shall not affect any actions taken by the designee or health care provider or records custodian prior to the date those persons or entities received the written revocation.

My health care provider cannot require me to sign this Authorization as a condition of providing medical treatment or continuing to provide medical treatment.

This Authorization expires on _____, or when the following event occurs: _____.

_____   _____
Signature of Patient/Authorized Representative   Date

Authority of Representative:
___ Patient is a minor and I am the patient's parent and natural guardian.
___ Patient is a minor and I am the patient's guardian, appointed by _____.
___ Patient is a ward and I am the patient's guardian, appointed by _____.
___ Patient is deceased. I am the patient's domestic partner, surviving spouse, executor, or administrator of the patient's estate, appointed by _____.
___ I am the patient's agent, designated in the patient's Health Care Power of Attorney.
___ I am the patient's attorney-in-fact, with the power to make the foregoing request under the terms of the patient's Durable General Power of Attorney and/or Durable Power of Attorney for Finances.
___ Other: _____.

This Authorization to Release Health Information and/or Medical Records is meant to conform to the requirements of a valid authorization as set forth in the Standards for Privacy of Individually Identifiable Health Information (the HIPAA Privacy Rule), 45 C.F.R. Parts 160 and 164. Section 164.508 describes these requirements.

**A PHOTOCOPY OR FACSIMILE OF THIS AUTHORIZATION SHALL
HAVE THE SAME EFFECT AS THE ORIGINAL DOCUMENT.**

APPENDIX B

Resources

B-1   Resources for the Lesbian and Gay Community
B-2   Countries Providing Benefits to Same-Sex Couples
B-3   Some Legal Benefits of Marriage
B-4   California Registered Domestic Partner Rights and Responsibilities Act of 2003
B-5   Vermont Civil Unions

Resources for the Lesbian and Gay Community

Legal Resources

1. Lambda Legal Defense and Education Fund

    A. National Office
       120 Wall St., Ste. 1500
       New York, New York 10005-3904
       (212) 809-8585 (voice)
       (212) 809-0055 (fax)
       http://www.lambdalegal.org

    B. Midwest Regional Office
       11 East Adams St., Ste. 1008
       Chicago, IL 60603-6303
       (312) 663-4413 (voice)
       (312) 663-4307 (fax)

    C. Southern Regional Office
       1447 Peachtree St., NE, Ste. 1004
       Atlanta, GA 30309-3027
       (404) 897-1880 (voice)
       (404) 897-1884 (fax)

    D. Western Regional Office
       3325 Wilshire Blvd., Ste. 1300
       Los Angeles, CA 90010-1729
       (213) 382-7600 (voice)
       (213) 351-6050 (fax)

    E. South Central Regional Office
       3500 Oak Lawn Ave., Ste. 500
       Dallas, TX 75219-6722
       (214) 219-8585 (voice)
       (214) 219-4455 (fax)

2. National Center for Lesbian Rights
   870 Market St., Ste. 570
   San Francisco, CA 94102
   (415) 392-6257 (voice)
   (415) 392-8442 (fax)
   http://www.nclrights.org

3. **National Lesbian and Gay Lawyers Association**
   20 East Lexington St., Ste. 1511
   Baltimore, MD 21202
   (508) 982-8290 (voice)
   (410) 244-0775 (fax)
   http://www.nlgla.org
   E-mail: info@nlgla.org

4. **Immigration Equality**
   Founded in 1994 and formerly known as the Lesbian and Gay Immigration Task
   Force, Immigration Equality seeks equal application of U.S. immigration laws
   toward lesbian and gay couples and are advocates for persons facing HIV/AIDS
   discrimination and those seeking asylum due to sexual orientation.
   350 W. 31st St., Ste. 505
   New York, NY 10001
   (212) 714-2904 (voice)
   (212) 714-2973 (fax)
   http://www.immigrationequality.org
   E-mail:info@immigrationequality.org

5. **Transgender Law & Policy Institute**
   Comprehensive transgender legal resource site.
   http://www.transgenderlaw.org
   E-mail: info@transgenderlaw.org

6. **Gay & Lesbian Advocates & Defenders (GLAD)**
   30 Winter St., Ste. 800
   Boston, MA 02108
   (617) 426-1350 (voice)
   http://www.glad.org
   E-mail: gladlaw@glad.org

Social Service Resources

7. **National Association of Professional Geriatric Care Managers**
   1604 N. Country Club Rd.
   Tucson, AZ 85716-3102
   (520) 881-8008 (voice)
   (520) 325-7975 (fax)
   http://www.caremanager.org

8. **Healthcare, Elder Law Programs (HELP)**
   Ed Long, Executive Director
   1404 Cravens Ave.
   Torrance, CA 90501-2701
   (310) 533-1996 (voice)
   (310) 533-1949 (fax)
   http://www.help4srs.org
   E-mail: questions@help4srs.org

9. **Human Rights Campaign**
   1640 Rhode Island Ave. NW
   Washington, DC 20036-3278
   (800) 777-4723 (voice)
   (202) 347-5323 (fax)
   (202) 216-1572 (TTY)
   http://www.hrc.org

10. **Love Sees No Borders**
    Dealing with issues affecting same-sex immigration in the United States.
    P.O. Box 60486
    Sunnyvale, CA 94088
    (413) 502-4758 (fax)
    http://www.loveseesnoborders.org
    E-mail: info@loveseesnoborders.org

11. **ACLU National Lesbian and Gay Rights Project**
    125 Broad St., 18th Floor
    New York, NY 10004
    (212) 549-2627 (voice)
    http://www.aclu.org/getequal/

12. **Gay and Lesbian Alliance Against Discrimination (GLAAD)**
    Promotes and ensures fair, accurate, and inclusive representation in the media.

    A. West Coast Office
    5455 Wilshire Blvd., Ste. 1500
    Los Angeles, CA 90036
    (323) 933-2240 (voice)
    (323) 933-2241 (fax)

    B. East Coast Office
    248 W. 35th Street, 8th Floor
    New York, NY 10001
    (212) 629-3322 (voice)
    (212) 629-3225 (fax)
    http://www.glaad.org

13. **National Gay and Lesbian Task Force (NGLTF)**
    Civil rights organization for the lesbian, gay, bisexual, and transgendered (LGBT) community.
    1325 Massachusetts Ave. NW, Ste. 600
    Washington, DC 20005
    (202) 393-5177 (voice)
    (202) 393-2241 (fax)
    (202) 393-2284 (TTY)
    http://www.ngltf.org

14. **Gay, Lesbian and Straight Education Network (GLSEN)**
    Provides information on establishing a safe school environment for LGBT students.
    121 W. 27th St., Ste. 804

New York, NY 10001
(212) 727-0135 (voice)
http://www.glsen.org
E-mail: glsen@glsen.org

15. **Parents, Families, and Friends of Lesbians and Gays (PFLAG)**
    National organization providing group support services for parents and friends.
    1726 M Street, NW, Ste. 400
    Washington, DC 20036
    (202) 467-8180 (voice)
    (202) 467-8194 (fax)
    http://www.pflag.org
    E-mail: info@pflag.org

16. **ABA AIDS Coordination Project**
    750 15th Street, NW
    Washington, DC 20005-1009
    (202) 662-1025 (voice)
    (202) 662-1032 (fax)
    http://www.abanet.org/irr/aidsproject

17. **BenefitsCheckUp**
    A free, comprehensive Web-based screening tool designed to match seniors to
    federal, state, and local benefits and services. The survey takes about 15 min-
    utes and is anonymous. The program then highlights programs the user may be
    eligible for and explains the application process.

    http://www.BenefitsCheckUp.org

18. **Gay and Lesbian Medical Association (GLMA)**
    459 Fulton St., Ste 107
    San Francisco, CA 94102
    (415) 255-4547 (voice)
    E-mail: info@glma.org
    http://www.glma.org/

19. **Kaiser Permanente**
    Provides a handbook on care that addresses LGBT issues, *A Provider's Handbook
    on Culturally Competent Care: Lesbian, Gay, Bisexual and Transgendered Popu-
    lation.*
    National Diversity Department
    One Kaiser Plaza, 22 Lakeside
    Oakland, CA 94612
    (510) 271-6663 (voice)
    (510) 271-5757 (fax)

20. **Joint Commission on Accreditation of Healthcare Organizations (JCAHO)**
    This organization evaluates and accredits hospitals nationwide. It provides the
    essential seal of approval that reflects the hospital's high performance standards.
    JCAHO has a system for reviewing complaints against an accredited health
    care facility. It will investigate the situation and recommend changes to prevent
    future repetition. Complaints can be mailed, e-mailed, or faxed. Submit a 1–2 page

summary describing the situation encountered and state your concerns. Identify the health care organization by name and address and try to identify the personnel with whom you dealt.
Hotline: (800) 994-6610
E-mail: complaint@jcaho.org
Office of Quality Monitoring: (630) 790-5636 (fax)

21. **Insurance for same-sex couples**
    Automobile:
       AETNA
       Commerce
       Hartford: (888) 466-9675; 35 states and Washington, D.C.
       Metropolitan
       Travelers

    Homeowners:
       Hartford: (888) 466-9675; 35 states & Washington, D.C.
       Allstate
       IDS/AMEX

    Renters:
       GEICO

22. **Family Caregiver Alliance**
    Seeks to improve caregivers' quality of life through education, services, research, and advocacy.
    690 Market St., Ste. 600
    San Francisco, Cal 94104
    (800) 445-8106 (voice)
    (415) 434-3388 (voice)
    http://www.caregiver.org
    E-mail: info@caregiver.org

23. **Association of Gay & Lesbian Psychiatric Referral Services**
    Referrals to gay or lesbian providers of psychiatric services.
    (215) 222-2800 (voice)
    http://www.aglp.org

24. **Mary-Helen Mautner Project for Lesbians with Cancer**
    Provides assistance for lesbians diagnosed with cancer.
    1707 L Street NW, Suite 230
    Washington, DC 20036
    (202) 332-5536 (voice/TTY)
    (202) 332-0662 (fax)
    http://www.mautnerproject.org

25. **National Association on HIV over 50**
    Resource site for persons diagnosed as HIV positive and over age 50.
    (816) 421-5263 (voice)
    (913) 722-2542 (fax)
    http://www.hivoverfifty.org

26. **Family Net**
    Section of Human Rights Campaign Web site deals with issues concerning lesbian, gay, bisexual, and transgendered families; source for gay-friendly senior housing.
    http://www.hrc.org/familynet

27. **List of health insurance plans for domestic partners.**
    http://www.gogay.net/insurlist.htm

28. **National Hospice & Palliative Care Organization**
    1700 Diagonal Rd., Ste. 625
    Alexandria, VA 22314
    (703) 837-1500 (voice)
    (703) 837-1233 (fax)
    http://www.nhpco.org

29. **Euthanasia World Directory**
    http://www.finalexit.org

30. **Organ Donations**
    The United National Organ Sharing (UNOS) is the agency coordinating organ donations. This group will *not* accept donations from gay donors due to a fear of HIV and AIDS. Some medical centers also prohibit gay donors for HIV and AIDS patients.
    http://www.organdonor.gov

31. **Source for life insurance for those who are HIV positive**
    http://www.HIVpositive.com

32. **Current information on individual state adoption laws**
    http://www.hrc.org/familynet/adoptions_laws.asp

33. **Lesbian and gay parenting resources**
    http://www.lesbian.org
    http://www.familypride.org
    http://www.queerparents.org
    http://www.familieslikeours.org
    http://www.ourfamily.org
    http://www.gayfamilyoptions.org
    http://www.colage.org
    http://www.pflag.org

34. **Association of Conflict Resolution**
    Mediation and arbitration.
    (202) 667-9700 (voice)
    http://www.acresolution.org

35. **COLAGE**
    International support organization for children with lesbian or gay parents.
    3543 18th St. #1
    San Francisco, CA 94110
    (415) 861-5437 (voice)
    (415) 255-8345 (fax)
    http://www.colage.org

36. **Lesbian and gay friendly therapists**
    http://www.glitse.com

37. **Senior Action in a Gay Environment (SAGE)**
    Activist lesbian and gay senior organization.
    (212) 741-2247 (voice)
    http://www.sageusa.org

APPENDIX B-2

Countries Providing Benefits to Same-Sex Couples

Current as of March 2004

1. Countries allowing same-sex marriage:
   a. Belgium
   b. Canada (as of 6/03; legislation pending in Canadian legislature to codify court decisions)
   c. The Netherlands

2. Countries providing benefits to same-sex couples:
   Australia, Canada, Denmark, Finland, France, Germany, Greenland, Iceland, New Zealand, Norway, Portugal, Porte of Spain, Sweden.

3. Countries recognizing same-sex relationships for immigration purposes:
   Australia, Belgium, Canada, Israel, New Zealand, Norway, South Africa, Sweden, United Kingdom (legislation pending in Parliament to grant same-sex couples marriage-like rights).

APPENDIX B-3

Some Legal Benefits of Marriage

Benefits during Lifetime
1. Make unlimited gifts to spouses without gift tax
2. Add spouse to real estate without incurring gift taxes or conveyance fees
3. Share in spouse's COBRA and net benefits
4. Be beneficiary of spouse on most employer-provided life insurance policies
5. Receive benefits under spouse's disability insurance policy
6. Be considered first for appointment as spouse's guardian or conservator
7. Make joint tax free gifts up to $22,000 per year to anyone
8. Revoke any reference to the spouse automatically upon divorce
9. Remove the spouse as beneficiary on retirement plans automatically upon divorce
10. Remove the spouse as nominee for guardian, conservator, or executor automatically upon divorce

Benefits at Death
1. Receive payments from the spouse's pension plan
2. Automatically roll over IRA proceeds to survivor without adverse tax consequences
3. Claim workers compensation survivor benefits
4. Claim unlimited marital deduction for tax purposes
5. Receive tax-free transfer of assets on death of spouse
6. Take advantage of both spouses' lifetime tax exclusion
7. Claim spouse's body/remains on death
8. Claim survivor benefits under Social Security
9. Claim homestead exemption on home
10. Claim intestate rights
11. Elect against the will of decedent spouse
12. Claim statutory spousal share if decedent spouse attempts disinheritance
13. Presume joint ownership of personal property
14. Presume equal ownership of jointly held property
15. Obtain bereavement leave
16. Have priority for appointment as executor of intestate estate

APPENDIX B-4

California Registered Domestic Partner Rights and Responsibilities Act of 2003

The new law (Assembly Bill 205) takes effect on January 1, 2005. In order to be covered by the new law, couples must register with the State of California. Registration with a city, county, or other state is insufficient to be covered by this new law. The registration fee under the new law is $10.

Couples presently registered with the state who do *not* want to be covered by the new law must file a Termination of Domestic Partnership form with the California Secretary of State.

The Declaration of Domestic Partnership form is available from any county clerk's office or from the Secretary of State's office. Forms can be downloaded from the Secretary of State's Web site, http://www.ss.ca.gov. The phone number of the Secretary of State is (916) 653-3984.

Same-sex partners must be at least eighteen years of age. For opposite-sex domestic partners, one must be sixty-two or older.

There is no specific residency requirement under the new law. The law requires only that the couple share a common residence. There is no requirement that the residence be in California.

The new law provides the following rights, duties, and obligations to registered domestic partners in California. These are identical to the rights, duties, and obligations provided to married couples in California:

- Rights and duties of support during the partnership
- Rights and duties of support after termination of the partnership
- Fiduciary duty between partners
- Right not to be excluded from your partner's dwelling (house/residence)
- Right to damages for attempted murder
- Restriction on altering relationship by contract, except as to property
- Joint ownership of property acquired during the partnership, with rights of survivorship
- Joint obligations for debts incurred during the partnership
- Protection under rent control laws
- Equal management and control of property acquired during the partnership
- Protection against assignment of partner's wages
- Homestead protection against creditors of surviving partner after death of declared owner
- Property interests governed by federal law (e.g., patents and copyrights)
- State constitutional guarantees for protection of separate property
- Presumption of parenthood regarding child born during the partnership or through alternative insemination

- Judicial determination of custody and support of children born during the partnership
- Ability to authorize medical treatment of partner's children
- Right to control disposition of remains, authorize autopsy, make anatomical gifts, and authorize exhumation
- Right to be buried in joint or family cemetery plot
- Identification of partner on death certificate
- Provisions for handling inheritance after simultaneous death of partners
- Protection of survivor's interest in joint property following partners' death
- Protection against disinheritance by partner
- Ability to avoid probate of jointly owned property
- Ability of surviving partner to collect compensation provided to victims of violent crime
- Availability of presumptions protecting interests of surviving partner under workers compensation
- Right to take extended unpaid leave to care for a partner
- State government hiring preference for surviving partners of veterans and partners of disabled veterans
- Right to use any necessary force to protect partner from wrongful injury
- Ability to request and obtain absentee ballots for partner
- Ability to appear on behalf of partner in small claims court
- Ability to defend partner's rights in certain civil actions
- Ability to obtain notice that partner is being involuntarily held in mental institution
- Ability to obtain notice that partner who is a parolee or probationer has certain medical conditions
- Privilege for confidential communications among partners
- Privilege not to be forced to testify against partner
- Right to sue for loss of consortium
- Right to sue for violation of right of publicity of deceased partner
- Right to recover damages against employer liable for partner's wrongful death
- Right to sue person who provided illegal drugs to partner
- Ability to obtain tax treatment that takes relationship into account (partial rights)
- Exemption from transfer tax on deed or other writings transferring, dividing, or allocating joint property among partners pursuant to termination of the relationship
- Right of franchisee to designate surviving partner to operate franchise
- Joint interest in fishing permit
- Ability to inherit partner's commercial fishing license
- Ability to inherit license to run driving school
- Ability to obtain transfer of deceased partner's special license plates
- Ability of veteran's surviving partner to succeed on pending application for farm or home purchase
- Partial exemption from license fee on mobile home or trailer coach owned by and constituting principal place of residence of surviving partner of veteran
- Consideration of partner's income and need for support in determining student financial aid
- Exemption of current or former partners from requirements upon transfers of real property

- Prohibition on acceleration of mortgage on transfer to partner
- Coverage of partner as an insured under auto insurance policies
- Tuition fee exemption for surviving partners of veterans
- Education assistance for surviving partners of victims of September 11, 2001
- Eligibility for Medi-Cal payments if partner is in a nursing facility
- Access to married student housing
- Authority to use car rented by partner if licensed and of sufficient age
- Ability to obtain overnight visitation with partners who are in prison
- Certain employees' entitlement to leave of absence after death of partner
- Protection of partner's interest in public employer's retirement benefits and pension
- Right to continued health coverage and benefits after death of public employee partner
- Right of surviving partner of a deceased legislator to collect benefits
- Right to be buried in state burial ground if partner is a legislator
- Death benefits for surviving partners of firefighters and police
- Scholarship of surviving partners of firefighters and peace officers
- Prohibition on certain crimes against, and disclosure of residences or phone number of, partners of certain public officials and employees
- Exclusion of gifts from partners from limitations on judge's receipt of gifts
- Coverage of partners in laws governing conflicts of interest by certain government officials based on personal relationships with parties
- Exclusions of interest in the income of one's partner from certain conflict of interest laws
- Coverage of relationship under conflict of interest rules governing Coastal Commission members and employees
- Coverage under state laws prohibiting discrimination based on being or not being in the legal relationship
- Rights and obligations relating to, and assistance in resolving disputes regarding, division of property, support, and other matters when the partners have children or significant property or debts or have been long-term registered partners

Assembly Bill 25

Assembly Bill 25 went into effect in January 2002. As of July 2003, domestic partners can inherit a portion of the deceased partner's intestate estate. One-third to two-thirds of the intestate estate will belong to the blood relatives.

Effective July 1, 2004, domestic partners will be able to take paid employment leave to care for a seriously ill domestic partner or child of that partner. This leave is also available with birth, adoption, or placement of a foster child with the couple. The employee will be able to collect 55 percent of salary while on leave with a maximum of $728 per week for a period of six weeks.

Seniors living in senior citizen housing have the right to live with their registered domestic partner. The surviving domestic partner also has the right to continue living in the residence after the death of the senior citizen.

There is a California law that prohibits a person who prepares a will or trust from receiving any assets under that document. This law will not apply to domestic partners.

APPENDIX B-5

Vermont Civil Unions

Vermont law permits certain benefits and protections that are comparable to the rights granted married couples. Vermont laws using the words "spouse," "family," "dependent," "next of kin," and "immediate family" apply to same-sex couples.

Only same-sex couples can enter into civil unions. The parties must be unrelated, over eighteen years of age, and mentally competent and cannot currently be in a civil union or a marriage.

Some of the benefits and obligations for same-sex couples entering into civil unions are

- Partners are responsible for supporting each other
- Relationship is governed by state law on annulment, divorce, separation, custody, support, property division, and maintenance
- Couples can hold real estate in Vermont as "tenants by the entirety"
- Partners are treated as spouses for purposes of inheritance and probate laws
- State health insurance is available
- Spousal abuse protections and programs are available
- Partners are covered by laws involving workers compensation
- Medical care and hospital/nursing home rules apply in the same way as with married couples
- Couples are covered by the Vermont family-leave benefits
- Couples can qualify for public assistance
- Partners cannot be required to testify against each other
- Couples are entitled to benefits of special Vermont laws for veterans and family farmers
- A child born to either party during the relationship is considered the natural and legal child of both partners

INDEX

A

Accelerated benefits, 17
Acknowledgment of representation, 40
Administration on Aging, 84, 85
Adoption, 10, 12, 63
  second-parent adoptions, 25, 27, 35, 36,
    64, 66–68
  wills and, 31–32
Advance directives, 15–16, 73–75, 82
Affidavits, 15
Agent designation, 17, 75, 138–139
Aging. *See* Seniors
Agreements, 12–13, 19–28. *See also*
    Domestic partnership agreements;
    Shared-parenting agreements
  buy-sell agreements, 78, 104
  joint representation agreements, 120
  right of first refusal agreements, 104
Agriculture payments, 11
AIDS/HIV, 82, 110
AIDS Task Force, 110
Alabama, 67
Alaska, 55, 67
Aliens, 11
Alimony, 10
Alternate residue clauses, 31
American Arbitration Association, 24
American Bar Association, 112
  Family Law Section, 63
American Express Financial, 18, 105, 113
Annuities, 99–100
Appointment letter, 118–119
Arbitration, 24
Area Agencies on Aging, 84–85, 86
Arizona, 81
Assisted living facilities, 84, 85, 101–102
Attorney-client privilege, 10
Attorney-client relationship, 3–6
Authorization for medical care, 71, 140,
    144–145
Authorization of visitation, 75
Autopsies, 75

B

Bank accounts
  joint tenancy of, 56
  payable-on-death accounts,
    57–58
Beneficiaries, 99
Benefits
  accelerated, 17
  children and, 36
  countries providing, 185
  employment benefits, 11
  government benefits, 11–12
  health insurance benefits, 5, 14, 63,
    66, 69
  legal benefits of marriage, 186
  living benefits, 17
  public benefits, 82
  Social Security benefits, 10, 11, 63, 66,
    69, 79, 82, 90, 98
Best Friends, 45
Bide-A-Wee Golden Years Retirement
    Home, 45
Birth control, 87
Body, claim to, 9
Breach of personal services contract, 77
Burial determination, 9
Bush, George W., xv
Business powers of attorney, 78
Business relationship, 98
Business succession, 104
Butterworth, Bob, 83
Buy-sell agreements, 78, 104

C

California
  intestate succession statutes, 29
  legal protection of LG couples, 7, 19, 20,
    187–189
  second-parent adoptions, 67
  seniors, 22, 81, 89
  sexual relationships, 23
  transfer-on-death vehicle certificates, 61

California Registered Domestic Partner
    Rights and Responsibilities Act of
    2003, 187–189
Canada, 103
Cemeteries, 77
Census data, 1, 81–82
Charitable remainder annuity trusts, 46
Charitable remainder trusts, 45–46
Charitable remainder unitrusts, 46
Checklist for estate planning, 147–148
Child care, 27
Child support, 10, 12, 27
Children, 8, 13, 63–72
    benefits and, 36
    child's best interest, 64, 69–70
    custody rights, 10, 12, 66
    as dependents, 27
    determining parents of, 65
    difficult issues, 69–70
    guardian appointment, 10, 35–36, 68, 69,
        70, 77, 141–143
    health insurance for, 27, 63, 66, 69
    life-planning issues, 71–72
    number with GL parents, 63
    psychological parent, 70–71
    questions to ask, 65
    school problems, 71–72, 144–145
    second-parent adoptions, 25, 27, 35, 36,
        64, 66–68
    shared-parenting agreements, 25–28,
        65–66, 167–170
    standby guardian, 68
    testamentary provisions, 68–69
    travel with, 71
    visitation rights, 10, 12, 27, 63, 69, 70
    wills and, 31–32, 68–69
Church teachings, 103
Civil rights laws, 19
Civil service benefits, 11, 79, 99–100
Civil Service Retirement System (CSRS), 79,
    99–100
Civil unions, 8, 19, 20, 102–104, 190. See
    also Vermont civil unions
    Social Security and, 88–89
    tax returns and, 97
    versus marriage, xiii–xiv
    wills and, 29
Claim to the body, 9
Client estate planning checklist,
    147–148
Collaborative law, 24
Colonial Apartments (Florida), 86
Colorado, 44, 67, 70

Comfort level, 3–4, 5
Conflict of interest, 11, 40
Connecticut, 19, 50, 67
Consent for medical treatment, 140,
    144–145
Constitution, U.S.
    First Amendment, 70, 103
    Fourteenth Amendment, 103
    full faith and credit clause, xiv, xv, 25,
        102, 103
    marriage amendment, xv, 103
Consumer Reports, 85
"Contemplation of death" category, 59
Contract breach, 77
Contract law, 13, 22, 76
Contracts, 19–21. See also Domestic
    partnership agreements; Shared-
    parenting agreements
Credit accounts, 97
Credit reporting agencies, 96
Credit reports, 95–97
Crimes, 11
Crooks v. Gilden (1992), 23
Cruzan v. Director, Missouri Dept. of
    Health (1990), 17
CSRS (Civil Service Retirement System), 79,
    99–100
Custodial care, 90
Custody rights, 10, 12, 66

D
Daniel, Robert, 16
Death taxes, 49–51. See also Estate taxes
Debts, 95–97
Deeds
    transfer-on-death deeds, 61
    warranty deeds, 30
Defense of Marriage Act (DOMA), 1, 10,
    11, 47, 97, 98
Delaware, 67
Demography, 63
Dependents, 27, 97–98
Designation of agent, 17, 75, 138–139
Designation of heir proceedings, 32–33
Disability insurance, 93, 105
Discretionary trusts, 41–43, 91
Discrimination, 5, 82, 83, 86, 101
Dissolution of relationship, 10, 12, 24,
    165–166
District of Columbia, 50, 58, 67
"Do Not Resuscitate" (DNR) orders, 74
Doctor bias, 87
Document customization, 5

DOMA (Defense of Marriage Act), 1, 10, 11, 47, 97, 98
Domestic partnership agreements, 21–25
   additional clauses for, 173–174
   complex, 150–158
   separate property, simple, 159–161
   shared property, simple, 162–164
   termination of partnership, 12, 24, 165–166
Domestic Relations law, 103–104
Due process, 70–71
Durable powers of attorney, 132–136
   for finances, 77–78
   springing, 78, 137

E
Educational expenses, 48, 49
Educational seminars, 112–113
Elder care, 17–18
Eldercare Locator, 85
Elderly. *See* Seniors
Emergency medical treatment, 63, 69
Employee Retirement Income Security Act (ERISA), 100
Employment benefits, 11
Employment policies of firm, 5
Equal Credit Opportunity Act, 97
Equifax, 96
ERISA (Employee Retirement Income Security Act), 100
Estate planning appointment letter, 118–119
Estate planning checklist, 147–148
Estate planning documents, 73–79
   business powers of attorney, 78
   designation of agent, 75
   durable power of attorney for finances, 77–78
   funeral arrangements, 75–77
   government accounts, 79
   guardian/conservator nomination, 77
   health care powers of attorney and living wills, 73–75
Estate taxes, 39–40, 47
   charitable remainder trusts and, 45–46
   jointly held property, 49
   life insurance and, 59
   state death taxes, 49–51
Executor, 34–35
   fiduciary duty, 76
   funeral arrangements and, 76
Experian, 96

F
Fair and Accurate Credit Transactions Act of 2003 (FACTA), 95
Fair Credit Reporting Act (FCRA), 95, 96
Family and Medical Leave Act, 64
Family law, 13
Family Law Section, American Bar Association, 63
Family Net, 63
Family status, definition of, 88
Family violence, 11
FCRA (Fair Credit Reporting Act), 95, 96
Federal Employees Retirement System, 79, 99–100
Federal Reserve Bank, 58
Federal Trade Commission
   Final Rule on Free Annual Credit Reports, 95
   Funeral Rule, 77
Filing status, 47, 97–98
Financial abuse, 82
Financial disclosure, 11
First Amendment, 70, 103
Flanigan, Bill, 16
Flanigan v. University of Maryland Medical System, 16
Florida, 30, 67, 81, 83, 86, 99
Focus groups, 109
Food stamps, 11
Foreign same-sex marriages, 102–104
Foster care, 10, 67, 68
401(k) plans, 83, 99
Fourteenth Amendment, 103
Full faith and credit clause, xiv, xv, 25, 102, 103
Funeral arrangements, 75–77

G
Gay Media Database, 111
Gay newspapers, 110–111, 113
"Gayby" boom, 2, 25, 63, 87
Gender-neutral language, 5
General Accounting Office (GAO), 11–12
Georgia, 23
Gift taxes, 14, 48–49, 61
   joint tenancy accounts and, 56
   life insurance and, 60
Goodridge v. Dept. of Public Health (2003), xiii, 4, 20–21, 29–30
Government accounts, 79
Government benefits, 11–12

Government retirement plans, 10, 79, 99–100
Government securities, 58
Guarantees, 11
Guardianship, 69
   guardian/conservator nomination, 77
   living trusts and, 38–39
   nomination, for adults, 171–172
   nomination, for estate and person of
      minor child, 141–143
   presumption of, 10
   psychological parents and, 70
   standby guardians, 68
   wills and, 35–36
Guardianship of Kowalski (1991), 39

H
Hawaii, 7, 67
Head of household, 98
Health and Human Services Department, 82
Health care, 10, 12, 14–17, 87
   dispensing medications, 101–102
   medical decisions, 9
   medical expenses, 17, 48, 49
   medical treatment authorization, 140,
      144–145
   mental health decisions, 10
Health care powers of attorney, 15–16,
      73–75
   guardian/conservator nomination, 77
Health insurance, 5, 14
   for children, 27, 63, 66, 69
   for seniors, 87, 93
Health Insurance Portability and
      Accountability Act (HIPAA), 17,
      74–75, 175–176
Heir proceedings, 32–33
Heirs at law, 8, 10
HIV/AIDS, 82, 110
Home health care, 101–102
Hospital visitation, 10, 12, 16, 63, 69, 73
Housing, 11, 86
Human Rights Campaign, 1
Human Rights Coalition, 63
Humane Society, 45

I
Illinois, 50, 67, 68
Immigration, 11
Immoral relationship, 23
In-home nursing care or assistance, 42–43
In re *Adoption of R.B.F. and R.C.F. and* In
   re *Adoption of C.G.G. and Z.C.G.*
   (2002), 67

In re Bonfield (2002), 64
In terrorem clause, 33
Incapacity, 56–57, 77–78
Incidents of ownership, 59
Incompetency, 38–39
Indiana, 50–51, 67
Indians, 11
Individual Retirement Accounts (IRAs), 49,
   83, 99
Inheritance, 10, 12, 63, 66, 69, 89
   heir proceedings, 32–33
   heirs at law, 8, 10
Initial estate planning appointment letter,
   118–119
Insurable interest, 59, 98
Insurance. *See also* Health insurance; Life
      insurance
   disability insurance, 93, 105
   long-term care insurance, 9, 18, 92–93,
      104–105
   seniors, 92–93
Intellectual property, 11
Inter vivos trusts, 40, 54
Internal Revenue Code, 37, 46
Internet, listings of LG publications, 111
Intestate succession statutes, 8, 10–11,
   29
Iowa, 50, 67
IRAs (Individual Retirement Accounts), 49,
   83, 99
Irrevocable life insurance trusts, 37, 46–47,
   60
Irrevocable living trust. *See* Living trusts

J
Joint accounts, 48, 92, 97
Joint Commission on Accreditation of
      Healthcare Organizations (JCAHO),
      16, 73
Joint representation agreements, 120
Joint tenancy, 54–57
Jointly held property, 49
Jones v. Estate of Daly (1981), 23

K
Kansas, 50
Kentucky, 50
Kowalski, Sharon, 39

L
Lambda Legal Defense and Education Fund,
   2–3, 16, 63, 86, 112
Lavender Law, 111

Lawrence v. Texas (2003), 4, 20, 23, 94, 112
Legal issues, 4, 7–18
    children, 13
    elderly, 17–18
    general issues, 8–9
    government benefits, 11–12
    health care, 14–17
    same-sex couples as legal strangers, 9–11
    taxes, 13–14
    written agreements, 12–13
Legal organizations, 111–112
Lesbian and Gay Community Centers, 110, 113, 114
Lesbian and gay legal organizations, 111–112
Lesbian and gay population, 1
Letters
    for drafts of documents, 127
    initial estate planning appointment letter, 118–119
    letter of instruction, 51–52
Liberty interests, 70–71
Life insurance
    avoiding probate, 55–56, 58–60
    children and, 98
    estate taxes and, 59
    gift taxes and, 60
    irrevocable life insurance trusts, 37, 46–47, 60
    Medicaid and, 92
    seniors and, 92, 93
    transferring ownership of, 59–60
    viatication, 17
Litigation, 2–3, 24
Living benefits, 17
"Living together" agreements. *See* Domestic partnership agreements
Living trusts, 37–40
    probate and, 38, 54
    retitling assets into, 54
    taxes and, 39–40
Living wills, 15–16, 73–75
Loans, 11
Lofton v. Kearney (2001), 67
Long-term care availability, 82
Long-term care insurance, 9, 18, 92–93, 104–105
Long-Term Care Ombudsman, 91
Look-back period, 90–91
Louisiana, 50, 58, 67
Lovers, as legal term, 23
Loving v. Virginia (1967), xv

M
Maine, 50
Marital status, and government benefits, 11–12
Marketing, 2, 5, 107–116
    books on, 109
    educational seminars, 112–113
    lesbian and gay legal organizations, 111–112
    newsletters, 113–115
    niche marketing, 109–111
    plan for, 108–109
    teaching, 116
Marrero, Lois, 83, 99
Marriage. *See also* Same-sex marriage
    constitutional amendment on, xv, 103
    Defense of Marriage Act, 1, 10, 11, 47, 97, 98
    legal benefits of, 186
    licenses, 103–104
    versus civil unions, xiii–xiv
Marvin v. Marvin (1976), 23
Maryland, 50, 67
Mashburn, Mickie, 83, 99
Massachusetts
    estate taxes, 50
    same-sex marriages, xiii–xv, 4, 7–8, 20–21, 29–30, 89, 97, 103
    second-parent adoptions, 67
    Social Security, 89
    taxes, 97
Mediation, 24
Medicaid and Medicare, 9, 82–83, 87, 89–92, 93, 98
    life insurance and, 92
    long-term care insurance and, 105
    look-back period, 90–91
    Medicaid payback trust, 42
    Social Security and, 90
    special needs trust and, 91
    transferring assets, 90–91
Medical decisions, 9
Medical expenses, 17, 48, 49
Medical information release, 17, 175–176
Medical treatment authorization, 140, 144–145
Medications, dispensing, 101–102
Mental health decisions, 10
Meretricious relationship, 10–11
Meretricious sexual services, 23
Military retired pay, 99, 100
Military service benefits, 11
Minnesota, 19, 50, 67

Mirror wills, 31
Miscegenation statutes, xv
Missouri, 61, 70
Mortgage deductions, 47

N
National Adoption Information
    Clearinghouse, 63
National Center for Lesbian Rights, 2–3,
    83, 86, 112
National Council on Aging, 84
National Family Caregiver Support
    Program, 84–85
National Lesbian and Gay Law Association,
    111–112
Native Americans, 11
Natural resources laws, 11
Naturalization, 11
Nebraska, 50, 67
Nevada, 67
New Hampshire, 50
New Jersey
    death taxes, 50
    legal protection for LG couples, 7, 20, 89
    pet trusts, 44
    second-parent adoption, 67
    Social Security, 89
New Mexico, 67, 81
New York
    death taxes, 50
    pet trusts, 44
    psychological parents, 70
    same-sex marriage, 103–104
    second-parent adoptions, 67
    standby guardians, 68
    transfer-on-death securities, 58
Newsletters, 113–115
Newspapers, gay, 110–111, 113
Niche marketing, 109–111
Niche practice, 2–3, 6
No-kill shelters, 45
Nomination of guardian
    for adult, 171–172
    for estate and person of minor child,
        141–143
Nondiscrimination policy, 5
North Carolina, 50, 58, 81
Notice of revocation of power of attorney, 149
Nursing care
    in-home care, 42–43
    skilled care, 90
Nursing homes, 10, 17, 82–83, 85–87, 90,
    101–102

O
OASDI (Old Age, Survivors and Disability
    Insurance), 88–89
Office environment, 5
Office of Long-Term Care Ombudsman, 86
Office on Aging, 83–84
Ohio
    death taxes, 50
    joint custody, 64
    prevalidating wills, 32
    retirement community, 81
    second-parent adoption, 68
    transfer-on-death vehicle certificates, 61
Oklahoma, 50
Old Age, Survivors and Disability Insurance
    (OASDI), 88–89
Older Americans Act, 84–85
Omnibus Budget Reconciliation Act of
    1993, 42
Oregon, 50, 67
Organ donation, 10
Ownership, incidents of, 59

P
Parental consent, for medical treatment of
    minors, 140
Payable-on-death (POD) accounts,
    57–58
Payable-on-death securities accounts, 58
Pennsylvania, 50, 67
Pensions, 10, 79, 83, 98–100
Persad v. Balram (2001), 103–104
Personal services contract, breach
    of, 77
Pet Estates, 45
Pet retirement homes, 45
Pet trusts, 43–45
Pets, 34, 43–45
Physical abuse, 82
Pick-up tax, 49–50
POD (payable-on-death) accounts,
    57–58
Population Association of America, 63
Population of U.S., 1
Pour-over provisions, 37
Powers of attorney
    business powers of attorney, 78
    durable powers of attorney, 77–78,
        132–136, 137
    health care powers of attorney, 15–16,
        73–75, 77
    revocation notice, 149
Presumption of guardian or conservator, 10

Priority of visitation language, 146
Prison visitation, 10
Privacy rights, 4, 74–75, 86
Probate, 10, 53–61
    joint tenancy, 54–57
    life insurance, 55–56, 58–60
    living trusts, 38, 54
    payable-on-death accounts, 57–58
    testamentary trusts and, 40
    transfer-on-death deeds, 61
    transfer-on-death vehicle certificates, 61
    Uniform Probate Code, 43
Property. *See also* Real estate
    divestment, 37
    division of, 10
    intellectual property, 11
    jointly held, 49
    lien on, 92
    transfer of interest, 37
Property tax reassessment, 55–56, 93
Prostitution, 23
Prudential Securities, 113
Psychological parent, 70–71
Public benefits, 82
Public speaking, 112–113
Publications, 111

Q
Queer Information Network, 111

R
Radio advertising, 115
Ramyard v. Ali (2002), 104
Real estate. *See also* Property
    charitable remainder trusts and, 46
    domestic partnership agreement
        and, 25
    joint tenancy, 54–57
    living trusts and, 38
    taxes and, 14, 25
    transfer-on-death deeds, 61
Referrals, 108, 112, 115
Release of medical information, 17,
    175–176
Religious same-sex marriages, 102–104
Representation, acknowledgment of, 40
Representing LG clients, 1–6
    benefits of, 6
    establishing a practice, 2–3
    expanding a practice, 4
    necessary changes in practice, 4–6
    preliminary considerations, 3–4
    underserved population, 1–2

Resources, 177–190
    California Registered Domestic Partner
        Rights and Responsibilities Act of
        2003, 187–189
    countries providing benefits to same-sex
        couples, 185
    legal benefits of marriage, 186
    for lesbian and gay community, 178–184
    Vermont civil unions, 190
Retirement
    communities and facilities, 81, 86,
        101–102
    Employee Retirement Income Security
        Act, 100
    government plans, 10, 79, 99–100
    IRAs, 49, 83, 99
    military retired pay, 99, 100
    pet retirement homes, 45
    retirement plans, 98–100
Reverse mortgages, 17
Revocable living trusts. *See* Living trusts
Revocation of power of attorney, 149
Rhode Island, 50, 67
"Right of first refusal" agreement, 104
Right of survivorship, 54
Russell v. Bridgens (2002), 67

S
Same-sex couples
    countries providing benefits to, 185
    as legal strangers, 9–11
    number of households, 1
Same-sex marriage
    constitutional amendment and,
        xv, 103
    foreign same-sex marriages, 102–104
    in Massachusetts, xiii–xv, 4, 7–8, 20–21,
        29–30, 89, 97, 103
    in New York, 103–104
    religious same-sex marriages,
        102–104
Savings bonds, 58
School problems, 71–72, 144–145
Schwerzler, Robert, 10–11
Second-parent adoptions, 25, 27, 35, 36,
    64, 66–68
Seminars, 112–113
Senior centers, 81
Seniors, 81–94, 101–102
    elder care, 17–18
    health care issues, 87
    insurance, 92–93
    Medicaid and Medicare, 89–92

Seniors (*continued*)
   numbers of, 81–82, 84
   nursing home care, 85–87
   Older Americans Act, 84–85
   Social Security, 88–89
Separate maintenance or alimony, 10
Severable clauses, 23
Sexual relationship, 22–23
Shared-parenting agreements, 25–28,
   65–66, 167–170
Skilled nursing care, 90
Slavery, xv
Smith, Sharon, 112
Social Security, 88–89, 98
   children and, 63, 66, 69
   civil unions and, 88–89
   Medicaid/Medicare and, 90
   as unavailable benefit, 10, 11, 79, 82
Social Security Act, 89, 98
Software, 4–5
Special needs trusts, 41–43, 91
Spendthrift trusts, 40–41
Sperm donors, 26–27, 66
Spouse, as legal term, 97
Springing durable power of attorney, 78, 137
Staff, 5–6, 109
Standby guardians, 68
Standing to sue, and funeral arrangements,
   76–77
State death taxes, 49–51
State Departments of Health, 87
State intestacy laws, 8, 10–11, 29
State law issues, 12
State tax liability, 35
State's rights, 25
Stress, 87
Successful Client Newsletters (Zwicker), 115
Succession
   business succession, 104
   intestate succession statutes, 8, 10–11, 29
Surrogate parents, 26, 65, 66
Survivor rights, 10
Survivorship rights, 54

T
T-bills, 58
Tampa Police Department, 83, 99
Tax returns, 97–98
Taxes, 11, 13–14, 47–51
   dependents, 27, 97–98
   educational payments, 48
   estate taxes, 39–40, 45–46, 47, 49–51, 59
   executor and, 34–35

filing status, 47, 97–98
   gift taxes, 14, 48–49, 56, 60, 61
   head of household, 98
   of health care benefits, 14
   IRAs, 49
   jointly held property, 49
   living trusts and, 39–40
   marital exemption, 47
   medical expenses, 48
   pick-up tax, 49–50
   property tax reassessment, 55–56, 93
   state death taxes, 49–51
   state tax liability, 35
Teaching, 116
Television advertising, 115
Tennessee, 50
Termination of domestic partnership, 10,
   12, 24, 165–166
Testamentary trusts, 40–45
   discretionary trusts, 41–43, 91
   pet trusts, 43–45
   spendthrift trusts, 40–41
Testator's attorney, suing, 31
Texas, 58, 67
   Lawrence v. Texas (2003), 4, 20, 23,
   94, 112
Thompson, Karen, 39
Thrift Savings Plan (TSP), 79,
   99–100
Totten trusts, 57–58
Trade, 11
Transfer of property interest, 37
Transfer-on-death deeds, 61
Transfer-on-death registration, 58
Transfer-on-death vehicle certificates, 61
TransUnion Corporation, 96
Travel
   with children, 71
   health documents and, 73
Trusts, 36–37
   charitable remainder trusts, 45–46
   discretionary trusts, 41–43, 91
   irrevocable life insurance trusts, 37,
   46–47, 60
   living trusts, 37–40
   Medicaid payback trusts, 42
   pet trusts, 43–45
   special needs trusts, 41–43, 91
   spendthrift trusts, 40–41
   testamentary trusts, 40–45
   Totten trusts, 57–58
   wills and, 37
TSP (Thrift Savings Plan), 79, 99–100

U

Uniform Probate Code, 43
Uniform Transfers-on-Death Securities
    Regulation Act, 58
Uniformed Services Former Spouse's
    Protection Act, 100
U.S. Administration on Aging, 84, 85
University of Maryland Medical System, 16

V

Vasquez, Frank, 10–11
Vasquez v. Hawthorne (2001), 10–11
Vehicle transfer-on-death registration, 61
Vermont civil unions, 8, 102, 190
    as domestic partnership agreement, 22
    legal protection for LG couples, 7, 19, 20
    second-parent adoption and, 67
    Social Security and, 88–89
    state death taxes and, 50
    tax returns and, 97
    wills and, 29
Veterans, 11, 82, 100
Veterans Health Administration hospitals, 82
Viatication, 17
Violence, 11
Virginia, 50
Visitation, 10, 12
    authorization of, 75
    children, 27, 63, 69, 70
    designation of agent, 75
    hospitals, 16, 63, 69, 73
    priority of visitation language, 146
Voting rights, xv

W

Warranty deeds, 30
Washington State, 10–11, 50, 67
Web sites, 111, 115

Webster v. Ryan (2001), 70
Westminster Oaks Retirement Community
    (Florida), 86
Whipple, Diane, 112
Whorton v. Dillingham (1988), 23
Wills, 4–5, 29–32
    adoption and, 31–32
    appointment of guardian, 35–36
    children and, 31–32, 68–69
    civil unions and, 29
    clauses to include, 33–34
    confidential will questionnaire, 121–126
    designation of heir proceedings, 32–33
    executor, 34–35, 76
    format of, 128–131
    funeral arrangements and, 76
    in terrorem clause, 33
    letter of instruction, 51–52
    living wills, 15–16, 73–75
    mirror wills, 31
    other considerations, 51–52
    prevalidating, 32
    trusts and, 37
Wisconsin, 19, 50, 67
Written agreements, 12–13
Wrongful death, 10

Y

Yellow Pages ads, 115

Z

Zwicker, Milton W., 115